The World of Allah

Morocco

Afghanistan

Egypt

Soviet Union

The World of Allah

David Douglas Duncan

Houghton Mifflin Company

Boston

Photography — Text — Design — Production
David Douglas Duncan

Printing & Binding
Dai Nippon Japan

Titles & Text Typesetting
Tokyo Ad Source

Master B&W Prints
Igor Bakhtamian

Map of Islamic World
Paul J. Pugliesi

Copyright © 1982
David Douglas Duncan

Houghton Mifflin Company
Two Park Street
Boston, Massachusetts
02108

ISBN
0-395-32504-8

Library of Congress
Catalog Card Number
82-6129

Quotations from The Koran
Translated by J.M. Rodwell
J.M. Dent & Sons Ltd.
London

First edition

Frontispage
Dusk in Old Cairo

Jerusalem
The Old City

Istanbul

Contents

Afghanistan

Preface

One of the ironies—perhaps tragedies—of our time is that almost nothing is known of the people and the lands that affect the lives of nearly everyone else on earth: Moslems, and their world of Islam. There are roughly five hundred million Moslems, who inhabit a vast arc of deserts, mountains, jungles, and seemingly boundless horizons stretching from the Atlantic Ocean to China and southward through Indonesia and the Philippines. In some countries, daily life has changed only slightly since the first appearance of the Koran, in the seventh Christian century, when Mohammed became recognized as the Prophet of Allah—God. Today, nomads still roam the steppes of central Asia, caravaners still navigate across the wilderness Sahara, and Bedouins still prod donkey trains through the serpentine back streets of Old Jerusalem, none of them much different from their ancestors who did the same thing, following the same routes, wearing almost identical garb a thousand—or two thousand—years ago. And, despite the impact of newly discovered oil under their deserts (if lucky) or being caught in the politics and violence of the new revolutionary fervor in their regions (if unlucky), the majority of the inhabitants of that enormous, often silent, usually harsh panorama are still endowed with humor and pride and simple qualities of the highest caliber: generosity and hospitality. I often shared both during a life of wandering far from my birthplace—the tranquil suburbs of Kansas City, where a camping vacation in nearby Colorado was treasured and considered high adventure.

For ten years after the end of World War II, leaving the Marines and becoming a *Life* photographer, I based in the Middle East, living in Cairo and Istanbul, Jerusalem and Tehran, and then in Rome from where I travelled to countries as widely separated as Spain and Indonesia. By design or accident, my camera assignments often dealt with Moslems. I photographed *The World of Islam* for *Life*—no accident—which then became a part of their series, *The World's Great Religions*. I also went on maneuvers with the Turkish cavalry on the Soviet frontier in the dead of winter (with riflemen assigned to protect me in the unlikely event—I felt—of attack by wolves from the surrounding forest), and they happened to be Moslems. In an attempt to thank Ibn Saud, King of Saudi Arabia and guardian of Mecca, Islam's holiest shrine, for both his patience and friendliness when I first photographed him, I, non-Catholic, gave him the St. Christopher medal that had been given to me when I went off to war in the Pacific. That battered silver image lay framed in the old king's desert-weathered palm as he peered at it with his one good eye before shoving it under his *abba*, with a nod and *"Ashkurak"* . . . "Thank you." No holy war! No Yankee-Protestant nomad skewered to the floor of his tent by bodyguards' daggers and swords. Several years later, when he died and the Kingdom was abruptly closed to foreigners, I arrived without a visa. I was in and out of jail, had photographed the new king (his son, Saud), and had shipped the films to *Life* in New York—all within three hours. It was that kind of world in which I lived and worked for so long, made possible by men who held hospitality to be sacred, nearly equal to life itself.

For weeks I made the tribal migration with the legendary Qashqais of Iran, living as a crown prince—with my own horse (or camel) and tent, washing each morning in a silver basin of warm water on which floated rose petals—four months after leaving the Marines. I photographed a circumcision on the Mount of Olives; a conversion to Islam in a remote Ugandan mud village; the Prophet's birthday parade in Malaya; the funeral ceremonies of an honored scholar in Indonesia. And I stood quietly beside praying Moroccans in the French army on the border of southern China, then photographed the Mecca-oriented graves of other Moslem soldiers who fell in the Indochina war. Later, I was to live with the Berbers in the High Atlas Mountains of northern Morocco, homeland of many of those troopers and surely *the* Shangri-la, if it exists on our planet.

This "diary" of a camera vagabond is only an introduction to one of the most photogenic and still challenging regions remaining on earth. Although several countries are today closed to foreigners, many of these photographs might have been taken yesterday; some probably could also be made tomorrow. And in that, these people and lands are unique.

We know, today, that the astronauts' boots pockmarked a celestial dead end, an ecological wasteland. Tomorrow's adventurer in the Moslem world will leave footprints in the living sands of history, witness the drama of many flamboyantly romantic yet crucial countries in ferment, and, if lucky, discover trails still worn deep by other stubborn nomads—the last of the free.

Five times a day throughout Islam, from Mauritania to Mindanao, orthodox Moslems are supposed—obliged—to stop whatever they may be doing and turn toward the Great Mosque in Mecca, ancient shrine-city of Saudi Arabia, to pray—bow, kneel, touch foreheads to earth—in silent communion with Allah. All believe in one holy book, the Koran, based on the disclosures and admonitions of God heard by His messenger and prophet, Mohammed. Islam's holiest celebration, Ramadan, commemorates that years-long period of divine revelations. The Koran also decrees laws, which guide the Faithful throughout life. Finally, unequivocally, it promises to reward the pure on earth with an eternity in heaven, embellishing this promise with inducements so sublime and humanly alluring that they perhaps dull the aura of other religions—or the appeal of those benefits, so often semi-worshipped, that result from today's materialistic Western and Japanese "work ethic." In many lands, an impression prevails that while daily existence may be searing and bleak for some among the devout Moslem multitudes, it is accepted as of little consequence since almost unimaginable serenity and treasure await the bodily famished but spiritually nourished. *"Malish!* . . . Who cares! Prayer, during this moment of hardship, is enough. Tomorrow is forever!"

And yet, I wonder. Certainly that image—almost a cliché—of abject submission to Fate would never pertain to the Moslems I met, or who were my friends, during ten years of meandering journeys in their homelands. Without disrespect or doubting the piety of religious persuasions of any Moslem—just as I would never question the depths of beliefs of any Catholic, Jew, Buddhist, Hindu, or Christian Scientist—I do question the ardor and submission to orthodoxy, said to dominate many of those half-billion infants of Islam who form their generation on our earth during this instant in mankind's narrative. Among all the Moslems I knew and worked with in one half of the world, it is difficult to recall any with traits singular enough to distinguish them from non-Moslems, equally close to me, from the other half of the world. Whether ordinary or remarkable, most were so casually tolerant, it seemed their religious convictions were eclipsed by other interests or were kept discreetly submerged and private as is so with nearly everyone, everywhere. Naturally, I have seen photographs of hundreds of thousands of pilgrims praying in the Great Mosque of Mecca (closed to nonbelievers), the dream of every Moslem. Seemingly endless flights of homing jumbo jets now reduce the pilgrimage—*hadj*—caravan or ship time to just hours, instead of the weeks, even months, needed by earlier generations of pilgrims. Increasingly, those jammed planes are unleashing the greatest flood of humanity ever to engulf a single site on an exact annual timetable. However, for many a pilgrim, that highly visible and often emotional outburst of religious fervor, is a once-in-a-lifetime escape—an austere, multinational jubilee shared with fellow believers who are generally of the same modest origins and livelihood as himself. Memories of the *hadj* must last forever. A veteran *hadji* is a rarity: restraints imposed by families, distances, and everyday realities are too great. For the pilgrim, praying in Mecca must be the ultimate reality—the vision, itself, fulfilled.

My introduction to the Moslem world nearly ended as abruptly as it began. Leaving the Qashqai nomads in summer pastures at the end of their migration to the mountain meadows west of Isfahan, I rolled my gift carpets—woven by sisters of the khans for their own family—and descended to the Mediterranean coast, to Palestine and a world with which I had recently been familiar: war. Jews, both native and refugees out of Hitler's charred Europe, had united finally to fight for their destiny. Their enemy—the British army—was in place under a League of Nations mandate, dated from the end of the First World War, when Palestine was sheared from a flank of the fallen Turkish Ottoman Empire. Poles, Russians, Czechs, Germans out of death camps, Hungarians, Romanians, a few French: weaponless, penniless, aflame with *the* dream: a homeland. Among them were scientist-statesman Chaim Weizmann, political infighter David Ben-Gurion, schoolteacher Golda Meir, and a will-o'-the-wisp, feared-above-all-and-by-all, skinny little streetfighter, Menachem Begin—leader of the Irgun Zvai Leumi underground commandos, who were hit-and-run attacking the British at every vulnerable point, using stolen and smuggled weapons and eye-for-eye brutality refined in the Gestapo-destroyed ghettos of Europe. The Palestinian Arabs, concerned but disorganized at that time, were townspeople, farmers, fishermen, Bedouins, and intellectuals—perhaps the most highly educated society in the entire Arab world. All were caught in the crossfire when the Irgun and the British set ambushes for the other.

To a young, just-out-of-uniform former Marine, it all seemed chillingly normal—with olive trees replacing mangroves and sunlight flaring off terraced limestone walls instead of brutalized coral beaches. Even the silhouetted machine-gunner in the back seat of a getaway car in Jaffa (Irgunmen were hitting the nearby Ottoman Bank for operating funds) seemed familiar, as he killed the three townsmen standing beside me.

He would have killed me, too, except he probably mistook me for a Sabra—Jew from a local kibbutz: faded khaki Marine shirt and pants, cropped dark hair, lean and still windburned to mahogany, as dark as any nomad or Zionist farmer. The killer spared—or missed—me, so I shot him, then my dead Arab neighbors and the wounded British bank manager, and the plainclothesmen and police and soldiers who had swarmed into that street corner. They nearly fired, too, thinking my flashgun-mounted Rolleiflex a weapon. *Life* published the pictures—as they had printed my coverage of the carnage and ruins after Irgun dynamiters blew up the King David Hotel in Jerusalem a few week earlier—a blast that claimed nearly one hundred random lives, military and civilian, Christians, Moslems, Jews. The King David was British headquarters. Eye for eye. In both *Life* stories, the Irgun were called "terrorists." At that time, living in the shadows of Weizmann and Ben-Gurion, surely no one could have imagined that Menachem Begin would one day be Prime Minister of Israel. But then, at that time, there was no Israel—only battlefields, and men like Begin. Many years later, he and his terrorists-now-heroes gathered to celebrate their victories—in the King David Hotel. Memories and history fade, or are rewritten; yesterday's violence soon muted. Other dreamers replace the fallen, and those fighters who age but survive. Palestine has always cradled its prophets and poets and dreamers; and fighters—some always survived. Former Irgun commander Menachem Begin, of all men, should have been the first to remember, the first to have tried to understand.

Ayatollah Khomeini was alone, idolizing hatred, dreaming of self-ordained purges for God; Yasser Arafat was unknown; Muammar Qaddafi a schoolboy; Anwar Sadat an ebullient aide trailing Gamal Abdel Nasser; and Nasser, himself, the *éminence grise* behind General Mohammed Naguib when King Farouk was dethroned. The young revolutionaries then streamed into the office of their father-figure friend and veteran diplomat, Jefferson Caffery, American ambassador to Egypt. They had won, yet were lost. They came seeking advice and books on governing a country. Nasser's colleague Ali Sabry put it bluntly: "We have Egypt. What do we do now?" I was in Cairo, in the embassy, in Caffery's office; and I saw and heard it all. Those young officers had no chance to run things American-style, with American support. Washington never listened—even to Caffery. He told me.

Some years later, when I resigned from *Life*, I was again in Cairo and went to say goodbye to Gamal Nasser, then President. It was he who gave me access to Farouk's palaces and the story on Gaza Strip now in this book—pictures taken when Gaza was closed to all but the Egyptian military. Upon finishing my orange juice and our visit, rising to shake hands and preparing to drive away into the spring desert night, I asked whether I might ask an extremely personal question, one that had plagued me for years after I took the first pictures of their revolution, from inside their own headquarters. My question was plain and simple: "Why have you never visited the United States?" His reply was equally direct: "I have never been invited." The next time we met, he flashed a smile and veered away from the lineup of welcoming officials to say hello. It was snowing, freezing. He looked as bulky and formidable in his great coat and black astrakhan hat as his host, Nikita Khrushchev. Atop their soaring towers, blood-ruby stars glowed in the swirling storm; above the treasury of crowns and thrones and cathedrals of the tzars I had been photographing when I heard that the President of Egypt had just arrived in town. He winced, but a half-smile returned, after I asked whether he was learning Russian: his English was fluent. The last thing I ever heard him say, was: "We're both a long way from home." Then he turned, to be driven into the Kremlin. I wondered where he would pray.

While living in Cairo, over many years I saw tens of thousands of Egyptians praying together in the first morning's dawn of Bairam, giving thanks for the new year. But normally, through the other months, prayer was a private rite, practiced alone. Exceptions had to be made under the impact of modern industrial forces, which drew large numbers of workers together during a long day, hours that spanned the regular times for prayers. I was never threatened for making photographs during prayers—pictures I felt were crucial to my coverage of Islam that were humiliating to take, as I would have felt if firing my camera during any religious service. In the oil fields of Saudi Arabia—one of the most idealistically pure of Moslem countries—I made photographs, supposedly proscribed, of those refinery hands who prayed during breaks in their work shifts. No one lifted a finger to menace me or my camera. Malaya, Indonesia, Turkey, Palestine, Algeria—the same: tolerance for a foreigner; and the sight of undulating masses of citizens praying, as rare as rain in the Sahara. It seemed that the average Moslem kept his religion invisible, like many of other faiths. Yet, for sheer shock and spectacle, few sects of any religion can rival the self-flagellating cults of Iran—fearsome and extreme— unless it be those rattlesnake-brandishing, Bible-embracing mountaineers of America.

I never saw a Qashqai, tribesman or khan, kneel in prayer; nor, apparently, did they dwell upon religion around their campfires. They talked about horses, rifles, hunting, and of other tribes. Favorite storytellers embroidered upon legends and the verbal history of their past. Those nomads, of course, filtered into Persia more than five hundred years ago from the steppes of Turkestan (they still spoke a Turkoman dialect among themselves) and probably abandoned a little spiritual luggage along the trail. Still, they arrived profoundly religious; at least their descendants are. They spoke with contempt of their roof-trapped, bazaar-oriented, Koran-waving, city-dwelling countrymen, whom they viewed as a race apart. And they often chuckled over earlier escapades of the youngest Qashqai khan, Khosro, who nearly got city religion at the source one afternoon in Tehran when he foolishly punched a young rival over the affections of a girl, then had to flee to his mountain home for his life—a raging Crown Prince Mohammed Reza Pahlavi in hot pursuit.

When with the Berbers, I recall seeing no one praying as I roamed their valleys and villages, or while tracking shepherds through alpine meadows and barren peaks. Still, they radiated a serenity of life and tolerance for each other that could only have been supported by a religion of pure refinement. Throughout Afghanistan, except for the few hundreds at prayers in front of Kabul's central mosque during national holidays, I saw no tribesman, shepherd, or nomad on his knees praying, despite being a people who faced Allah on the most intimate and sometimes terrifying terms during winter's blizzards and summer's whirlwind duststorms. In the sanctuary of the Dome of the Rock in Old Jerusalem, almost as sacred a shrine as the Great Mosque of Mecca itself, only a handful of elders sat in the sunswept southern portal while they murmured passages from the Koran, then, at the proper times, prayed. But of course, Palestinian Moslems, just as Palestinian Jews and Palestinian Christians, were born where part of their Faith was born, too. It was from the Holy Rock, in the Dome of the Rock Mosque, that Mohammed the Messenger and Prophet ascended to heaven when he answered the ultimate summons.

Leaving prayers and religion—and oil and politics and wars—in the Moslem world to others who wish to address those subjects in depth, this book is offered as the log of a wanderer's romance with an anchorless life, of my drifting toward an island of solitude that had beckoned since childhood—a mirage, discovered to be reality when I arrived among the nomads of Allah.

> For the nomad
> every morning
> of all seasons
> fills life
> with a promise
> of future dreams

Sunlight and Shadows

A Photographic Introduction to Islam

The oasis

Roots and hallowed traditions
of more than a thousand years
strengthen and enfold all Believers
whose Faith supports a world apart

Two thousand year-old olives

Palestine

Women in purdah

Pakistan

*Malik Mansur
Khan of the Qashqais*

*Shirazian plateau
Iran*

Bedouin shepherdess

Gaza — Palestine

*XIV-century Moorish king
ceiling mural on gold*

Spain

Images
of
an ancient era
remain unchanged today

XX-century Beersheba farmer
winnowing wheat

Palestine

Jerusalem

Sacred Shrine
of
Moslem Jew Christian

Dome of the Rock Mosque

Dome of the Rock Mosque

The Old City of Jerusalem

Reading from Koran

The Holy Rock ▶

Calls of the muezzin

The Old City of Jerusalem

XII-century windows
Gifts of Saladin

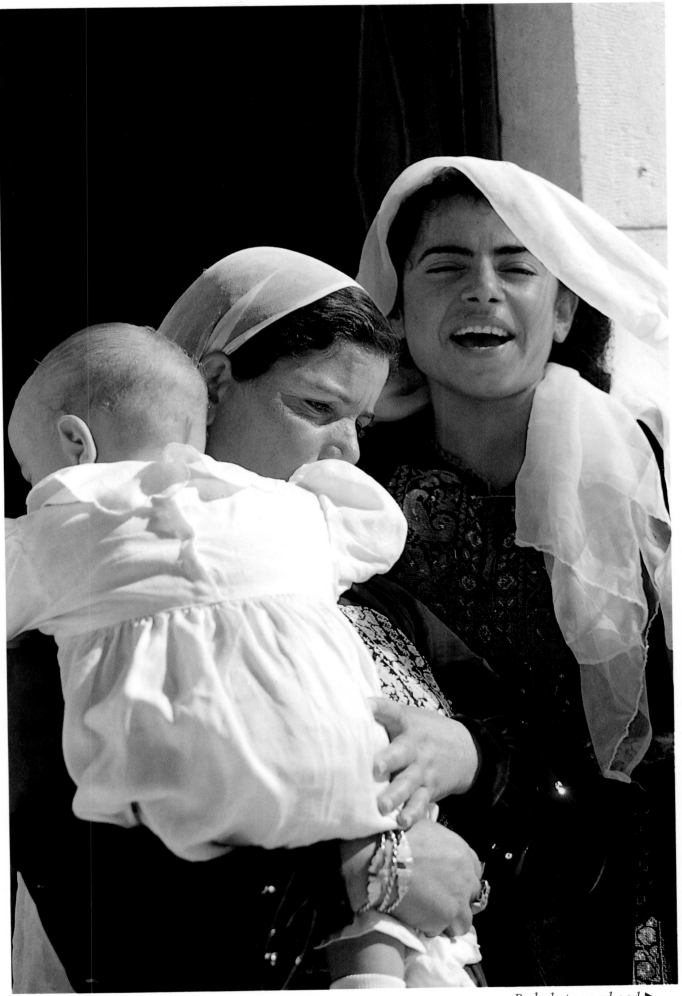

Pride of a mother

Prelude to manhood ▶

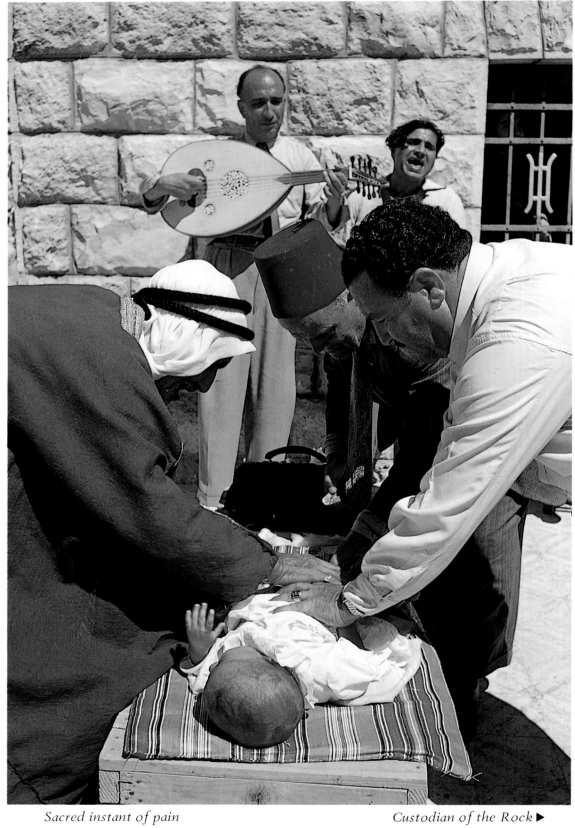

Sacred instant of pain

Custodian of the Rock ▶

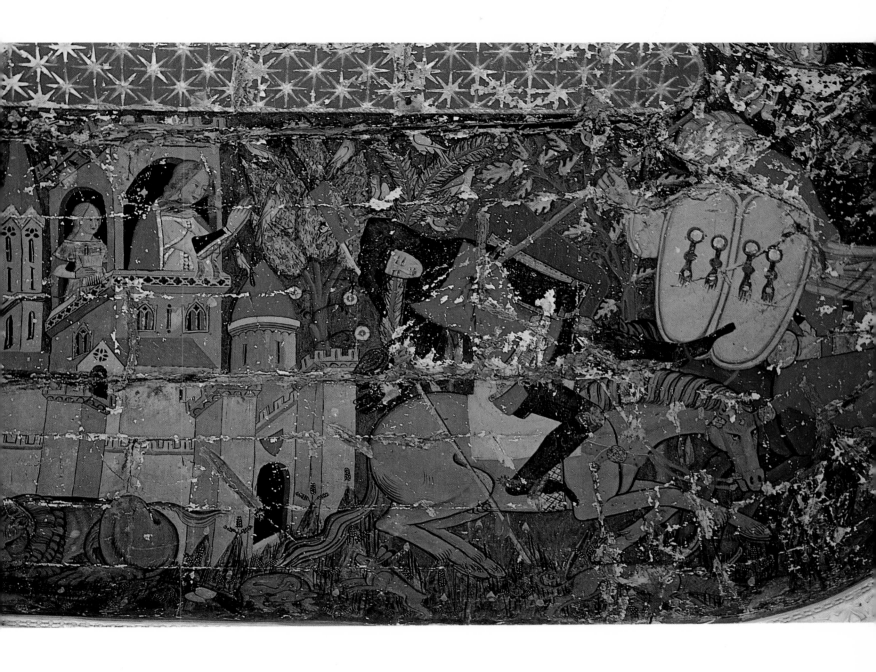

Spain

Ceiling murals celebrate epic legends
of princesses and kings
during the Moorish conquests

The Alhambra of Granada

◄*Courtyard tiles*   *Inner court*

A Fountain of Lions

Stone Script Everywhere

Forbidden Portraits on Gold

Hall of Ambassadors

Ceiling of Kings

The Great Mosque
of
Córdoba

Today a Catholic Shrine

Meeting of Two Worlds

The Berbers
of
The High Atlas Mountains

Morocco

Smile and tatoo

Brush cutter of Aït Attiq

Children of Shangri-la

The Upper Dadès River Valley

Worries of childhood
Aït Morrhad tribe

Zaïd and his lamb ▶
Aït M'Hand cemetery

Weekly ritual at Aït Tfeqirt

Burnoose laundry day

Wool spinners
Brush cutters

Berber Women

Saturday morning
Aït Tilmi

Adopted Saharan
Market-day matrons

Berber Men

Farmers and Shepherds

Market-day leisure

Aït M'Semrir

Souk Saturday

Aït Oussikis

Aït Attiq ▶

Aït Tfeqirt   *Family living room*

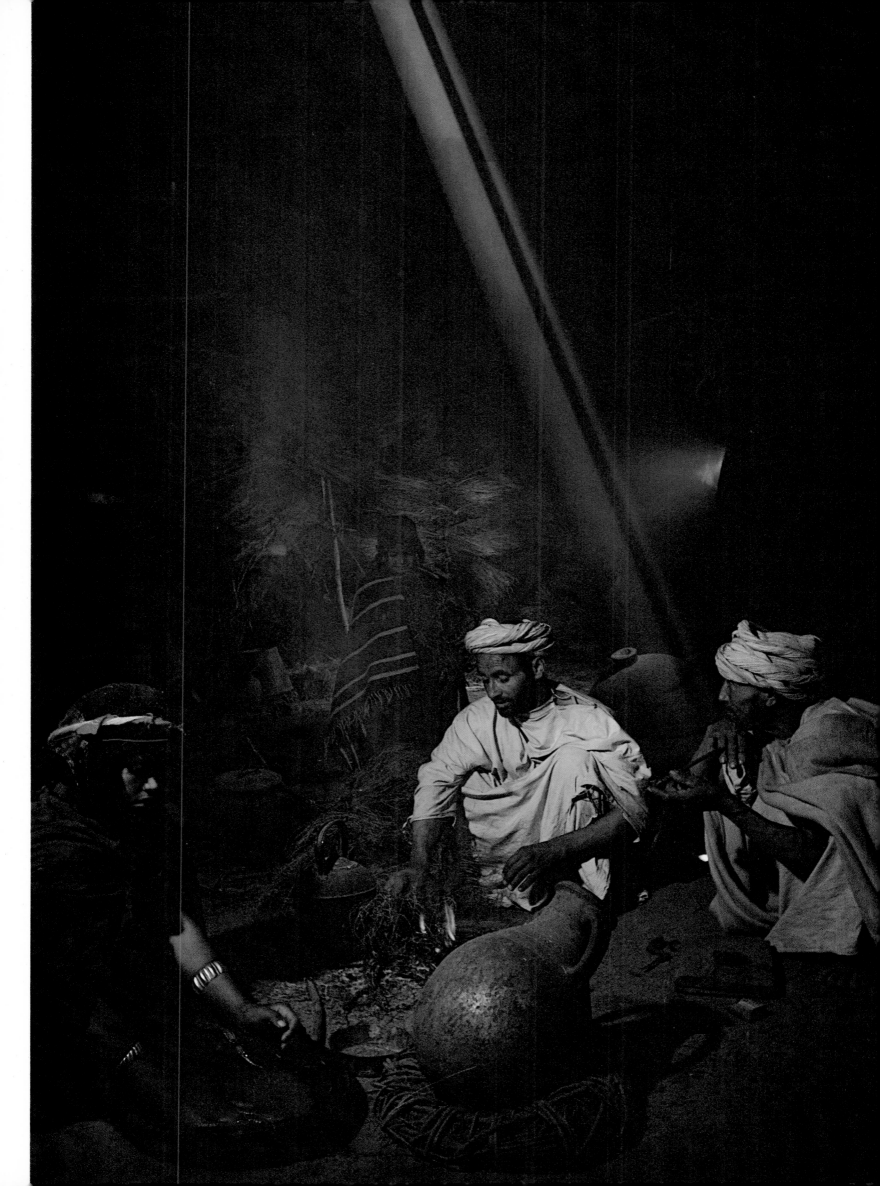

Aïcha M'Bark
Milling flour

Moha Ou Youssef
Saharan potter ▶

High Fashion
in
High Atlas Mountains

The trial
Adultry or rape?

Tribunal of Elders
Aït Hadiddou tribe

◀ *Lonely vigil*
 Idir the shepherd

Nightfall
Aït M'Hand

Paradoxes of Islam

Barefaced Women
of
The Atlas Mountains

Veiled Blue Men
of
The Sahara Desert

Village matriarch

Aït M'Semrir

Tuareg tourist caravan

Ahaggar Sahara Desert

Caravan commander
Tuareg nobleman Barka

Legends on the imzad ▶
Desert siren Tambarek

Two Thousand Years
of
Invaders and Conquerors

Roman Legions to Afrikacorps

Libya

Anguish of the ancients
Leptis Magna in ruins

Grave of yesterday's hero
Battlefield near Bardia

Bedouin's hitching post
Mussolini's rusting dream

89

"Venus of Garien"/Italian garrison wall
Clifford Saber/American Field Service

Graffiti of the Conqueror himself ▶
Eroding aqueduct at Leptis Magna

Tales of the hadj to Mecca
Rendevouz for Bedouin pilgrims

Children of the desert

Children
of
The City

Gazala and Karieh
Street Waifs of Tripoli

Egypt

Pageant of History

Pharaohs - Dervishes - Exorcists
Cannons of Ramadan - City of the Dead
Throne - Trash - Treasure
Legacy of a Fallen King

King Farouk's wedding present
Diamonds-and-gold coffee service

Royal grave robber
Pharaoh's burial mask

Lost Palaces
of
Playboy King

Ras el Tin Palace
Alexandria

Queen's bedroom ▶

Kubbah

Montazah

Ras el Tin

Farouk's Throne
Ras el Tin ▶

Scheherazade
Byzantine Room

Abdin Palace
Cairo

Whirling Dervish
Old City Cairo

Exorcists
Zar dancers

Mourning teen-age widow
Cairo's City of the Dead

Noontime Ramadan prayers
Cairo's Kasr el Nil bridge ▶

Daytime Fasting
Nightime Festivities
Dawn-to-dark Prayers

Ramadan

Mohammed Ali Mosque

Citadel of Old Cairo

Cannons and Prayers

Dusk of Ramadan   Dawn of Bairam

Abdin Palace Gates
Cairo's Republic Square

Women of Cairo

Prayers of Bairam

The Forgotten Land

Gaza Strip

Sardine fishermen of Gaza Beach

Sudanese asakir trackers

Dawn anti-smuggler patrol

Romance and Reality

Bountiful eternal sea
Pebbles for refugee huts

The honeymooners
Flowers in the sand ▶

Barber and Bedouin
of
Gaza Strip

Sudanese askari tracker
◀ *Sgt. Suliman Saleh Ahmed*

Mysterious mission
Gaza–Beersheba

Summer harvest

Gaza—Beersheba

The Shepherd

Salman Abu Atwa
Negev Desert Patrol

Spring planting

Hills of Bethlehem

Lifelong friends

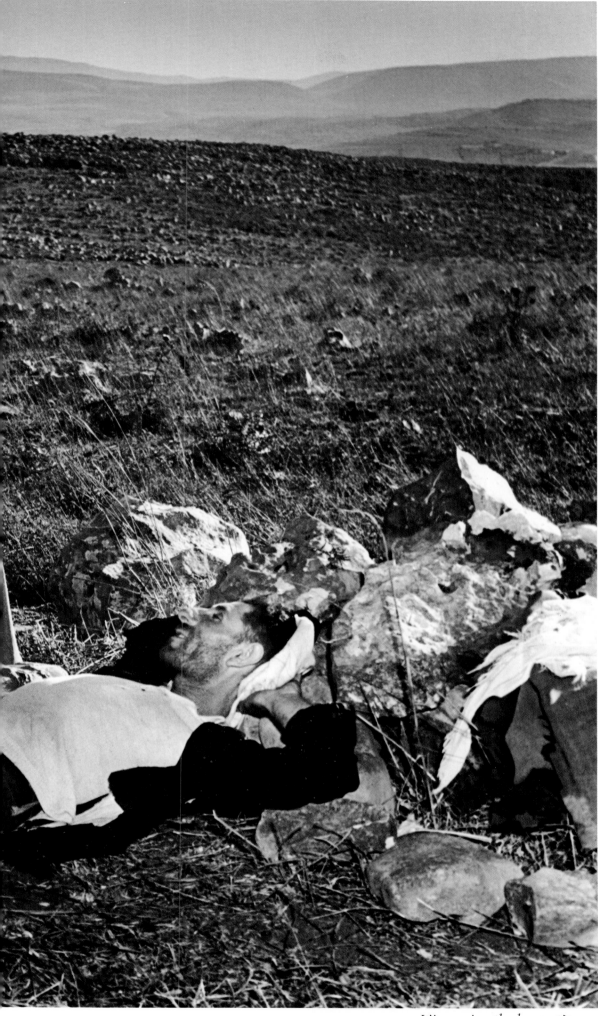

The Stones
of
Upper Galilee

Winnowing the harvest ▶

Turkey

The Bosphorus Straits

Crossroad of Conquerors

Moslem and Christian

Black Avni Mizrak
and
Toros

Two Thousand
Cavalrymen Disappear
into a
Blizzard
then
Forever

Ghosts in an ancient mirror
Maneuvers on Russian frontier

Malik Mansur Khan Qashqai

Iran

One Hundred Thousand Tribesmen
Move Tents to Summer Meadows

Asia's Medieval Spectacle
The Qashqai Nomads on Migration

The search for grass

Valley of Beaza

Every Trail
Every Mountain Pass
Every Stream
the
Stars - Moon - Sun
Have Been Companions
Since Childhood
of
Every Qashqai
Nomad

Descendants
of
The Horde
of
Genghis Khan

Faster!
Faster!
Ride Faster!

Nasser Khan Comes Here!

Today!

Khan of Khans
Mohammed Nasser Qashqai
his brother
Malik Mansur Khan
and
their nomadic tribesmen

Cavalcade
of
Yesterday

Tribesmen Acclaim Khan

Rejoin Migration

Await Autumn Hunting

Great Tent
of the
Khan of Khans

Summer Camp in Zagros Mountains

Subkhans and tribesmen

Nasser Khan Qashqai ▶

Nasser Khan at home
Carpets of Qashqai nomads

Nomad nobility
Khan Mother Khardijeh

Saudi Arabia

Tribesmen and townsmen

Forbidden Riyadh before OPEC

Bodyguards
of a
Bedouin Monarch

Saudis - Somalis - Sudanese

King Ibn Saud's tent

Dhahran on Persian Gulf

161

Reconciliation
of
Two Desert Dynasties

Abdullah King of Jordan
Descendant of The Prophet

Abdul Aziz Ibn Saud
King of Saudi Arabia

*Old Abdullah
Royal falcon master*

Royal palace rooftop banquet
Desserts and pastry for kings

Bedtime princely playthings
Grandfather's bodyguards' swords

One-half the Heirs
of
A Warrior-King

Another Eighteen Princes
Even More
Veiled Princesses - Baby Princes
Missed Their Big Brother's
First Photograph as King Saud
of
Saudi Arabia

First Day on Throne
King Saud Ibn Abdul Aziz

Great Majlis Hall
Khuzam Royal Palace

Remote Palace - Regal Prince

Miragelike Old Riyadh
soon to vanish
Mud bricks to Petro-billions

Desert nobleman Faisal
born to tragedy
Crown Prince - King - Murdered

Widows await King's coins
The road to Mecca before oil

Aramco derrick at Abqaiq ▶
Bedouin caravan to oblivion
173

Yankee nomad arrives in Riyadh

Yankee geologists burn-in Abqaiq 44 ▶

Mission newsboy
▼ *Mission muezzin*

Nigeria

Ahmadiyya Missionaries Explain Islam
Through Black Africa

"We are a very poor community
We have zeal
We devote our lives to our assigned tasks
We go willingly"

Teacher Hamzat Okunun

Lagos mosque-school

Maulana Mubarak Ahmed
Chief Missionary

Ahmadiyya Mosque
Nairobi

Kenya
and
Uganda

Missionary
Hakeem Mohammed Ibrahim

Three Thousand Miles a Year
Mountains and Jungles
On a Bicycle

Conversion Day

Christian
Vementura Mugasa
to
Moslem
Ismail Mugasa

The Dilemma

Christian and Two Wives
Convert . . . or Not?

Chief George Mogambwa of Nantabulirwa
Wife Namtebbe and Wife Nalwange

Hakeem Ibrahim advised reflection
Decision could await another day

Isfahan

Masjid Soltani

An Ethereal Bouquet of Tiles

Friday prayers
Leaves of autumn

Masjid Shah ▶
Alone with Allah

The King's Mosque

Ancient Skills Preserve Ancient Shrine

Masjid Shah

Pakistan

The Shadow World of Purdah

Women in burqas

Karachi

Hawks Bay holiday   *Karachi*

Behind the Veil

Pakistan Women's National Guard

Sharpshooter Zakia Sultana

Zeb-un-Nissa Hamidullah
Editor & publisher

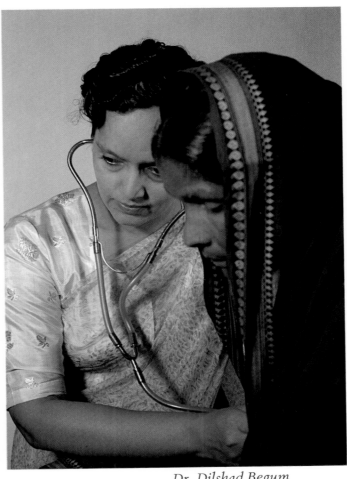

Dr. Dilshad Begum
Women's clinic owner

195

Raiza Khanum

*Pakistan Women's National Guard
Dominates purdah with flair*

Sughra Rababi

Pakistan Women's National Guard
Drives car and never in burqa

Kufic Koran

Mini-Koran

Islamic Museum
of
Egypt
Masterpieces

Mujur prayer rug

Soviet Union

Tadjik Chieftan

Painted Sand

May Day in Moscow

Afghanistan

Tribesmen and the Throne

Tatar wrestlers
Once-a-year gamblers
Roofs like girls' breasts
Ruins in the Desert of Death

Unorthodox orthodox Moslems
Five-dice gambling Afghans

Independence Day—from Britain
Jashan holidays in Kabul

Seven-man blockhouse
Facing the Red Army

Sacred blessing of Allah

Summer rain at Qal'eh Sarkari

There was a moment
in time
when it seemed
as another time

Camels of Imam Saiyid
Amu Dar'ya plateau

214

Earth was created
and then
God
gave it life

Uzbek farmer Murtazah Kul of Shibarghan
Roman-riding sons thresh wheat ▶

"It is God
who hath reared the Heavens
without pillars thou canst behold;
then mounted his throne,
and imposed laws on the sun and moon:
each travelleth to its appointed goal."

"He ordereth all things.
He maketh his signs clear,
that ye have firm faith
in a meeting with your Lord."

The Koran

Shepherd of Sar-e-Pul plateau

◀ *Rostan the Tadjik*
Wheat threshing

Hindu Kush Mountains
Lake Band-e-Amir

Faceless Buddah
Bamiyan

Lake Band-e-Amir
Mineral dikes ▶

The Hindu Kush

Lakes of Band-e-Amir

Tambourines - Paper Mosques
Silken Ladies - Silent Chinese

Malaya

The Prophet's Birthday Parade
Muar - Jahore

Ladies mourn apart

Indonesia

Death of a Hero in Djakarta

The Funeral of Hadji Agus Salim

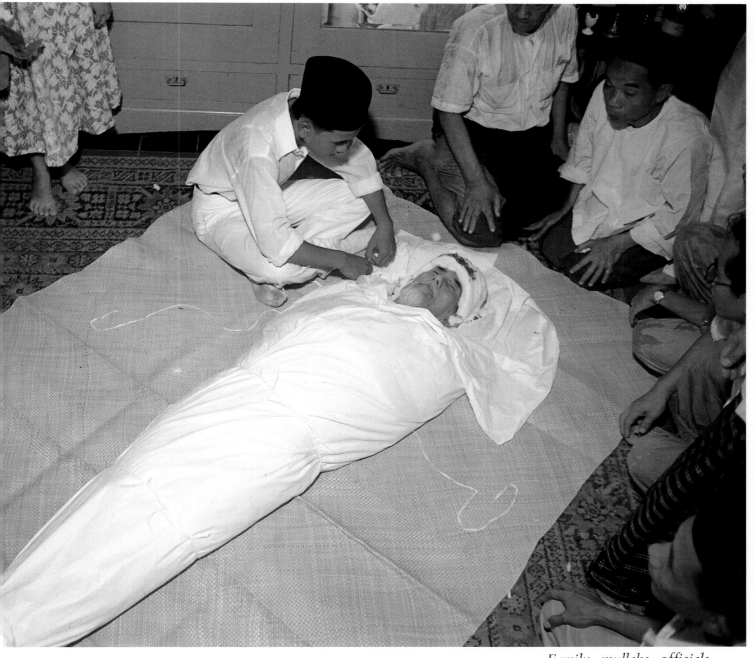

Family—mullahs—officials
Rituals to say goodbye ▶

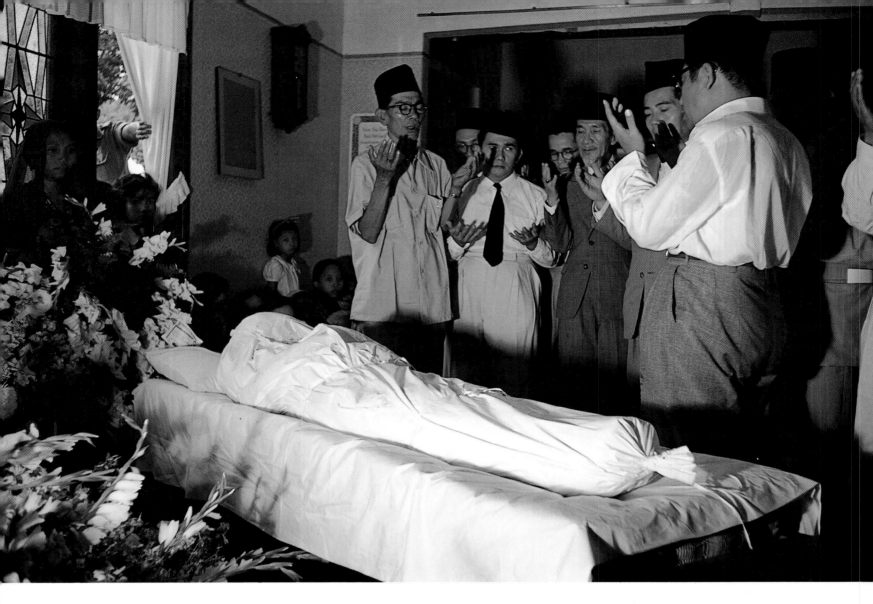

Three days national mourning

21-gun farewell salute

Makam Pahlawan
"Heroes Resting Place"

236

Indochina

French Military Cemetery

Hanoi Grave
of
Moslem Soldier

Birth through death
Every Moslem faces Mecca

Moslem and Christian graves
French Indochina War/Hanoi

And the servants
of the God of Mercy
are they who walk
upon the Earth softly;
and when the ignorant
address them,
they reply,
"Peace!"

The Koran

One silent voice
Indochina outpost

Evening prayers to Mecca
Across Communist China

No enemy sniper shot a Moslem
During moments after prayers

Suez
Canal

Dawn at Port Said

Fishermen
and
Freighters
of
Separate Worlds

Conceivably . . .
there was a grandson
of a great-grandson
of the grandson
of all the great-
grandsons
of Queen Nefertiti
whose portrait
helped sell handbags
in Port Said
three milleniums later

Moslem Women Mourn Alone
on
The Mount of Olives

They Pray in Old Jerusalem
at
The Dome of the Rock

Summer karakul sheep drive

Followed Trails of Ancestors
as They do Today

Mazr-e-Sharif Afghanistan

"Do ye indeed disbelieve in Him
who in two days created the earth?
and do ye assign Him peers?"

*Nomadic Zey-Yeds
Bow only to Allah*

Descendants of the

"The Lord of the worlds is He!"

Mohammed in Mecca

The Koran

Dedicated
to the Qashqai nomads
who shared their far horizons
family tents and solitude
with another nomad
from Missouri

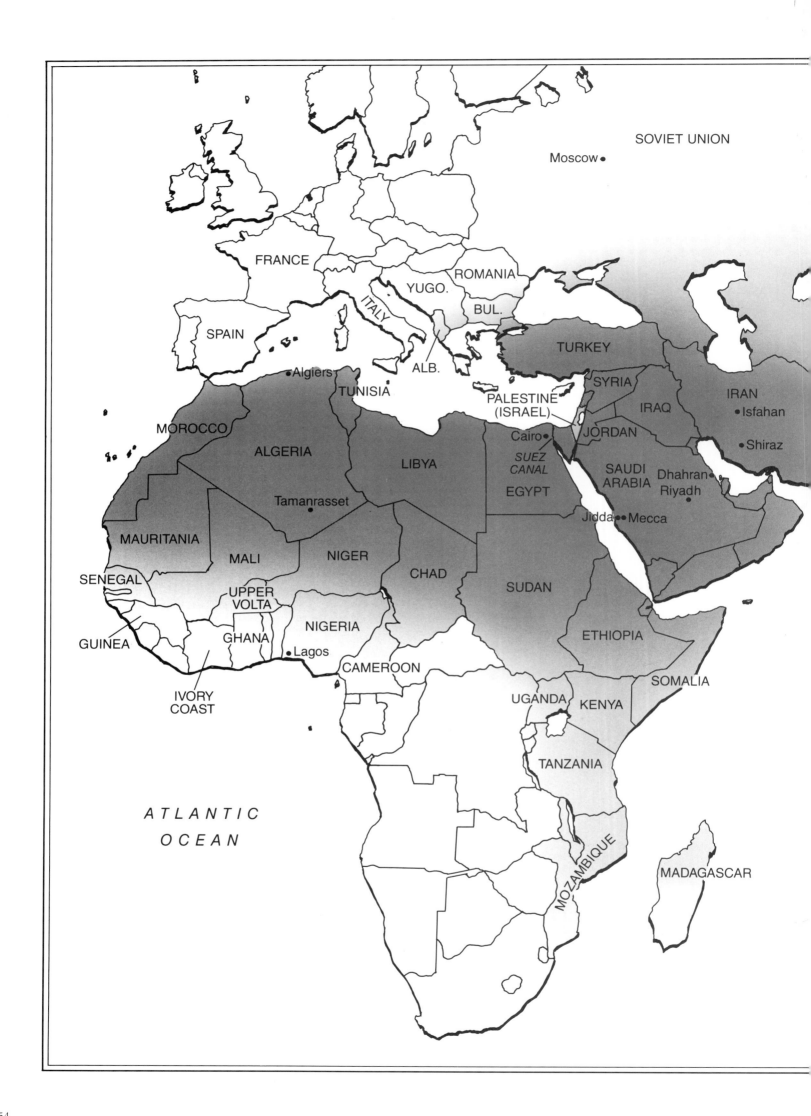

SOVIET UNION

Moscow •

FRANCE

ROMANIA

YUGO.

BUL.

ITALY

SPAIN

ALB.

TURKEY

SYRIA

IRAN

• Isfahan

• Algiers

TUNISIA

PALESTINE
(ISRAEL)

IRAQ

MOROCCO

Cairo •

JORDAN

• Shiraz

ALGERIA

LIBYA

SUEZ
CANAL

SAUDI
ARABIA

Dhahran •

EGYPT

Riyadh •

Tamanrasset •

MAURITANIA

Jidda • • Mecca

MALI

NIGER

SENEGAL

UPPER
VOLTA

CHAD

SUDAN

GUINEA

GHANA

NIGERIA

ETHIOPIA

SOMALIA

IVORY
COAST

• Lagos

CAMEROON

UGANDA

KENYA

ATLANTIC

TANZANIA

OCEAN

MOZAMBIQUE

MADAGASCAR

254

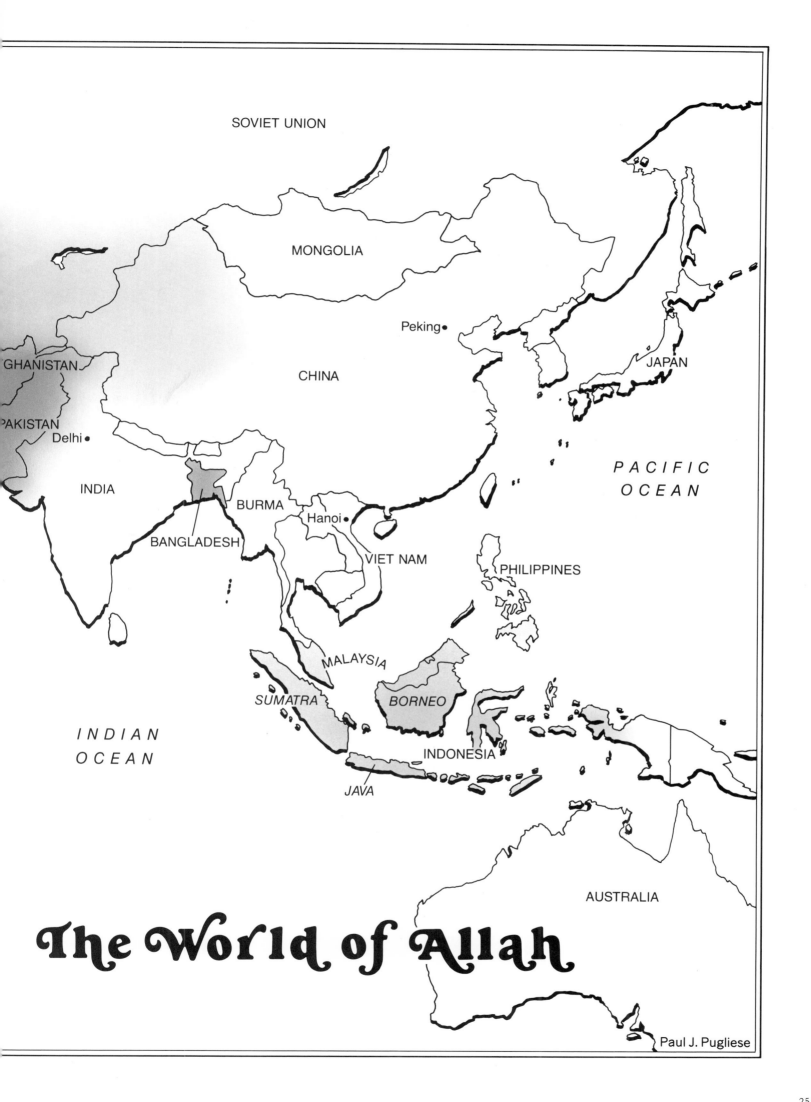

The World of Allah

Paul J. Pugliese

He it is who ordaineth
the night as a garment,
and sleep for rest,
and ordaineth the day
for waking up to life.

The Koran

He will say,
"What number of years
tarried ye on earth?"
They will say,
"We tarried a day,
or part of a day;
but ask
the recording angels."
God will say,
"Short indeed was the time
ye tarried,
if that ye knew it."

Photo Data

Front endpaper A: Moorish Caliphs of Spain during the Arab conquests were painted on a golden ceiling in "The Hall of Kings" of the Alhambra, in Granada, where they still are today. Adjacent alcoves reveal lovelorn princesses awaiting warrior-knights, several of them already fatally skewered on enemy lances. Lions drowse in the Andulusian sunlight and jewelled birds preen in treetops. All were painted by artists whose origin is now a mystery. Granada fell in 1492 and the Moors were driven back into North Africa—just as Colombus was discovering America. *(see pages 26, 39 & 43)*

Front endpaper B: Bedouin matriarch of tribal shepherds in Gaza Strip. *(page 123)*

Page 1: Berber children of Morocco in the High Atlas Mountains, near the village of Aït Attiq where their mother had left them at home while cutting fuel brush in the distant foothills. The distinctive black-white-red-striped serapelike cloak, chin tatoo, love of regal colors, direct gaze, and fair complexions distinguished them as members of the Aït Morrhad tribe—like all Berbers of the High Atlas, perhaps of prehistoric Aryan origin. *(pages 48-80)*

Pages 2-3: The Valley of Band-e-Amir. A solitary Afghan tribesman washes before prayers as first sunlight touches the upper canyon walls, while mineral-laden mist veils the dawn sky. Band-e-Amir (Lake of the Amir), in the central Hindu Kush (Hindu Killer) Mountains, is created by great mineral springs of almost freezing water—even in summer—which emit no fumes of nauseous hydrogen sulfide, generally synonymous with mineral springs. The lake itself is contained behind the lower cliff at left, over which a waterfall cascades. Minerals manufacture the retaining dikes behind which the lake (lakes, actually, since there is a chain of five) continues to rise above the valley floor, as eons of mineral-saturated deposits raise the natural dams ever higher. Band-e-Amir is one of the little-known wonders of the world. *(pages 221, 223, 224-225)*

Pages 4-5: Zar dancers in the Old City of Cairo, gyrate among the minarets of Sultan Hassan and Sultan Ahmed mosques. Zar dancing is a ceremony similar to voodoo originating in the Upper Sudan. Many people of the Nile Valley believe that evil spirits *(sheikhs)* can be cast into a person by someone wishing him ill. To neutralize or eliminate the *sheikh* demands zar dancers, who belong to a band of itinerant professional exorcists known as Abou-Gheit, a cult shunned by orthodox Moslems. They wear their hair as long as a woman's and most movements are accomplished without moving the feet. The body is swung in fast and ever-faster circles, often bending from the waist, until the torso, arms, head and hair are just a blur. Not a sound is uttered. Musicians force the tempo, playing the *tableh* (drum), *hana* (tambourine), and *saffara* (flute). Zar dancers rarely discuss calls asking them to visit the old quarters of Cairo and more remote villages where superstitions are still strong, because cures involving animistic rituals such as theirs are frowned upon, or banned, in much of modern Islam. Yet, in distant regions of the Nile, zar dancers are said to be still in constant demand. There, after hours of spinning and twisting, they sink into inert heaps upon the sand—itself considered a part of the cure and a good omen, for in their comas they are believed to be closer to an ecstatic contact with Allah. *(page 105)*

Pages 6-7: Tadjik tribesmen from Central Asia parade their horses across a carpet of painted sand in Moscow to help celebrate May Day festivities. The multihued pattern is achieved by sprinkling dyed sand into an enormous waffle-ironlike wooden grid, which recreates the design for the next day's pageant. *(page 199)*

Page 8: Dusk of Ramadan in Old Cairo. Fringes of lights atop minarets of Sultan Hassan Mosque announce the end of that day's abstinence, after the evening cannons of Ramadan have been fired. *(page 110)* The mosques of Rifai and Mahmoudiah loom against the evening desert sky. Sultan Hassan was built in 1356. Although not one of Egypt's oldest mosques, it is considered a masterpiece of Islamic architecture.

Page 11: The Old City of Jerusalem: Bible—Torah—Koran; Mohammed—Jesus—Moses . . . even Solomon; Saladin—Richard the Lion Hearted—Lawrence of Arabia; The Mufti—Weizmann—Count Bernadotte—Begin—Arafat . . . and more. The Old City of Jerusalem—so much more for so many more.

Page 12: Minarets of great mosques, Haghia Sophia and Sultan Ahmet, dominate the skyline of Istanbul's Golden Horn. A water taxi carries its passenger toward kayiks sailing from all over the Aegean, bringing cargoes of grain, wool, timber, fruit and tobacco to be unloaded at the wharfs of the ancient city's Galata Bridge. Byzantium—Constantinople—Istanbul: dream in the hearts of Crusaders, thorn in the hearts of Popes, obsession in the hearts of Tzars, jewel-of-jewels in the hearts of Sultans, lodestone of mystery in the hearts of novelists . . . end of the vision for Alexander the Great, whose sarcophagus is still there.

Pages 14-15: Afghan shepherds lead their flock along the Markhane River where it cuts valleys in the dreaded (by foreign invaders) Hindu Kush Mountains, the barrier that frustrated and blocked the greatest conqueror himself, Alexander, during his thrust toward India. *(pages 200-227)*

Page 16: Malik Mansur, Khan of the Qashqai nomads of Iran, descendant of Genghis Khan, lord (with his three khan brothers) of 30,000 square miles of deserts, mountains and meadows—and dominant force-by-migration over another 50,000 square miles; fluent in four languages, graduate of law from Oxford; at home either on horseback or in his ever-moving cluster of multicolored tents. *(pages 140-155)*

Page 21: The oasis near Beersheba where Bedouins and local Arab farmers rest during the midday heat, either going to or coming from the market in town: watermelons, woolen carpets, local wheat, imported dates and coffee.

Page 22: Arab townsman walks the long road back to Gaza, through tremendous olive trees that have lined the way since before the birth of Mohammed, perhaps since before the birth of Christ.

Page 23: Moslem women in purdah—wearing their *burqas* in the Old Delhi balloting place during the 1947 referendum that partitioned British India into Moslem Pakistan and Hindu India; an historic moment, which also became the major monument over the grave of Britain's colonial empire, with Last Viceroy Lord Louis Mountbatten leading the cortège.

Page 24: Chief bodyguard of King Ibn Saud during the monarch's visit to Aramco's oil field operations at Dhahran, on the Persian Gulf. Unblinking, burning eyes, magnificently embroidered cashmere *keffies* and *abbas* (and gold-and-bejewelled swords and daggers, and pistols and rifles and bandoliers of bullets) set the King's protectors apart from all other men in the desert. *(pages 160-161)*

Page 25: Bedouin shepherdess on the edge of the Negev Desert, between Beersheba and Gaza, wears treasured heirlooms while tending her family's flock of goats and sheep. Her tiara of coins came mostly from now-forgotten regimes of the Middle East; her necklace was of glass beads from—to her—foreign towns, and of amber, quite possibly the sacred souvenir of an ancestor's then hazardous pilgrimage across the Arabian Desert to Mecca.

Page 26: Portrait of a fourteenth-century Moorish caliph of Spain, painted on gold-on-leather and seen, today, on the illuminated ceiling of the Alhambra in Granada. In most countries embracing orthodox Islam, portraits and realistic images were forbidden subjects for the artist of the major, Sunni, sect. Artists of the Shi'ite sect—a minority—developed the painting of miniature portraits, hunting scenes, and even idealized romantic love stories to unimagined heights, images unsurpassed today. Whoever painted the ceiling themes found in the Alhambra is now unknown. *(Front endpaper A, pages 39, 43)*

Page 27: The dignity of daily work, and an affection for the yield of the earth, seemed to frame the universe of this patrician-profiled old Palestinian winnowing wheat, whose silhouette exactly mirrored the turbaned profile of the Moor painted five centuries earlier on a palace ceiling in Spain. No refugee or Bedouin, this man, whose ancestors had lived on the same land in Palestine—Gaza Strip—for countless generations, since the beginning of recorded history.

Page 28: The Old City of Jerusalem at sunset, silhouetted through the northwest *mawazeen* (an arched, free-standing, open-topped wall) that flanks the Dome of the Rock Mosque. The *mawazeen*—"scales"—is the place for weighing Moslems' souls on Judgment Day. Cupolas and belfries of Christian churches loom over squat stone houses and shops, and unlighted streets, unchanged for centuries, until the Arab-Israeli wars.

Mecca, as the birthplace of the Prophet Mohammed and thus the birthplace of Islam, ranks as the keystone of the Moslem faith; also because Mohammed designated the *Kaaba* (square shrine protecting a sacred black meteorite) in the center of the city, as the focal point of his new religion and the magnetic pole for all prayers. Until that decree, believers of his infant faith prayed toward the Rock of Jerusalem, long a hallowed place. Every Prophet since Abraham had worshipped there, and it was from there that Mohammed flew to heaven guided by the Angel Gabriel who had disguised himself as Al-Buraq, the Prophet's battle-veteran Arabian stallion. Before the sacred night's journey, Al-Buraq was tethered to the Great Wall of Solomon's destroyed Temple, holy of holies for Jews—West Wall—the "Wailing Wall." Thus, two of the world's great religions have roots entwined deep beneath Old Jerusalem's bitterly fought-over hills and shrines.

Page 29: The lead-sheathed dome of the Dome of the Rock (before recent restorers embellished it with gilt), surrounded by its mosaic-encrusted outer arcades, and protective wall. Most of the vivid blue, white, and yellow tiles—geometric designs and Arabic verses from the Koran—were added in the sixteenth century by the Turkish Sultan, Suleiman the Magnificent. The colors and patterns resemble the finest prayer rugs, not surprising considering their origin. Major damage was inflicted during the first Arab-Israeli war of 1948; tiles shattered, stained-glass windows destroyed, inner ceilings blasted and torn apart. A few tiles, and one stained-glass window, have survived from the first day, in 691, when the mosque was consecrated. Historian Aref-el-Aref believes that the Dome of the Rock is the world's oldest example of Moslem architecture.

Pages 30-31: The Dome of the Rock and the Old City of Jerusalem, seen from the Mount of Olives, east of the mosque. In the foreground, above the trees of the Garden of Gethsemane, is the Russian Church of Mary Magdalene. The eastern *mawazeen* rises as an open portal above the steps of the shrine. Ochre, beige, and olive blend in muted harmony with the barren slopes of Palestine—until shimmering desert sunlight illuminates the vast *haram* (rectangular compound) of limestone that surrounds the mosque; flagstones polished smooth by countless sandaled feet of Jerusalem's worshippers, and foreign pilgrims.

There is no earth more revered by a greater variety of faiths, than this austere Mediterranean hilltop. For Moslems, it is second in holiness to Mecca and Medina, where Islam and the Koran were born. The Stations of the Cross of Jesus are here. Abraham raised his hand here to sacrifice his son Isaac—atop the Rock itself—and Noah's Ark, in Islamic lore, touched here after the Flood. And here, too, is that mighty ruin of immense brooding stones of Solomon's Temple—and Herod the Great's—both "Wailing Wall" and "Al-Buraq," to Jew and Moslem. Moslems also learn that Allah sent His angels to the Rock, before creating Adam.

Venerable though it is—Moslems have prayed here for thirteen hundred years—Dome of the Rock is the most recent holy edifice to be erected and adored on the same mystical place. David, perhaps first, prayed and built an altar upon the great Rock; his son, Solomon, raised his temple around 940 B.C., and the vaulted catacombs still to be seen are said to have been his stables: they served again for horses when the Crusader Templar Knights arrived two thousand years later. Nebuchadnezzar demolished King Solomon's Temple in 586 B.C. It was replaced by another in 515 B.C., which was destroyed and replaced by still another, of Herod the Great, in 20 B.C. Emperor Hadrian leveled that one in A.D. 135, then built his own, probably utilizing the ever-deepening debris.

Hadrian's Temple stood unmolested for two centuries—fleeting moments in the history of the sacred hillock—until Queen Helena, mother of Constantine, Rome's first Christian emperor, visited Jerusalem and ordered the demolition of all pagan shrines and idols. Residents of Jerusalem, indifferent to its awesome past, made a trash heap of the devastated area for three hundred more years. Then Omar, second Caliph of Mecca, captured the city. He was so appalled by what he saw, he personally helped clear away the polluting refuse . . . and, in 636, ordered the construction of a mosque atop the Rock itself to commemorate the bit of earth where the Prophet answered Allah's summons—soaring into the night sky astride Al-Buraq, returning to that miraculous Rock before dawn. Finally, fifty-five years later, in 691, a visionary named Abdul-Malek saw the fulfillment of one of mankind's noblest dreams silhouetted against the sapphire desert sky.

The Dome of the Rock, in the Old City of Jerusalem, unchanged since the seventh century, is today still a sanctuary of fathomless serenity for Moslems—and visitors of other faiths—who pray for its safety and survival during these times of savage one-week wars in a now unholy land.

Page 32: The south door of the Dome of the Rock serves as a sunny rendezvous for elderly worshippers as they read the Koran. Double arcades encircle the mosque, under ceilings painstakingly repainted through the centuries to preserve their original seventh-century motifs. The enormous carpets were donated to the mosque by the Turkish Sultan, Abdul-Hameed II, at the end of the nineteenth century. Eight marble columns and sixteen pillars support the domed ceiling. Many experts believe they came from the ruins of Constantine's church, wrecked by Persians in 614. Other historians think some of the columns came from Herod the Great's temple, demolished by Emperor Hadrian in the second century after Jesus walked through the same narrow streets of Jerusalem that exist today.

Page 33: The Rock is an outcropping of limestone that measures 58 by 44 feet (17.7 meters, east to west and 13.5 meters, north to south). During the early occupation of Jerusalem by the Crusaders, priests chipped off fragments of the stone and sold them to pilgrims, reportedly for their equal weight in gold. Later Crusaders raised an iron grille to prevent such sacrilegious vandalism. Saladin left it intact when he entered the city, and it still encloses the Rock today.

The Christians also placed a cross atop the dome and an altar upon the Rock, which Saladin quickly obliterated. Beneath the Rock is a grotto, where Moslem Believers' souls are assembled on Judgment Day and where most of the Prophets of Islam, Judaism and Christianity have prayed. The blood of Isaac would have joined that of other martyr-victims here, had Abraham sacrificed his son—fanatical sacred blood flowing down through the gaping hole in the stone, to seep into the earth below . . . a darkening stain to enshrine one soul's eternity.

The reliquary beside the Rock contains two hairs from the Prophet Mohammed's beard . . . venerated as earthy evidence of the visit, here, by a desert man who heard the voice of Allah.

Page 34; top: Sheikh Omar Azaz, 72, chief muezzin of the Dome of the Rock, calling residents of Old Jerusalem to noontime prayers from his minaret high above their rooftops. After sixty years in the mosque, and five times daily climbing the dark spiral staircases of minarets, Sheikh Omar began to view with considerable interest a high-powered public address setup with loudspeakers that would reach the entire Old City, making obsolete his lifelong calls toward each of the four cardinal compass points. Bells—disdained by Mohammed—are unknown in mosques, perhaps because of their association with Christianity and Buddhism. Minarets, even formal mosques themselves, were architectural additions and refinements that appeared in Islam after the death of Mohammed, in 632. The Prophet himself apparently considered *anyplace* proper and adequate for prayers. His home in Medina, before the fall of Mecca and dispatch of resident pagans, was reportedly a modest affair little better than a Bedouin hut—all he needed for living, or prayers. It, of course, soon became a holy spot, a shrine equal to the *Kaaba* of Mecca.

Page 34; bottom: Saladin, in the twelfth century, installed stained-glass windows in the Dome of the Rock, perhaps influenced by reports of the artistry seen in windows of cathedrals where the vanquished Crusaders prayed when at home. Unlike cathedral windows, which elaborated upon Biblical themes, Saladin's artists developed abstract designs of pure colors, avoiding the human figure—or any figurative subject—believed to be proscribed by the Koran.

Page 35: Announcing to neighbors on the Mount of Olives the circumcision celebrations of an infant son, mother and aunt herald the rites for seven-month-old Salah Abu Riche. The child was the youngest addition to the family (6 sons and 3 daughters) of Arab refugee camp director Ibrihim Abu Riche, whose ancestors have lived in Bethany, on that rocky hillside, since before written records were kept by town officials.

Page 36: Male relatives and neighbors of the Abu Riche family gathered on the front porch of Ibrihim's stone-walled home during the circumcision rites, first to dance then to witness the event itself. Womenfolk of the family and neighborhood gathered in the yard of another member of the clan (a few hundred yards away) also to dance. There was no mixing of sexes until after the operation—which only the mother and a few aunts attended. The old *mukhtar* (mayor) of Bethany, Hadji Chahadeh el Qatir (also uncle of the Abu Riches), wears camel hair *abba* (robe), silk *keffie* (head scarf), and black goat-hair *akal* (head band). The *mutaher* (doctor), Ezat el Mograbeh, in red tarbouch, had cared for practically all of Arab Jerusalem and the surrounding towns at circumcision time for years. The father assisted, as musicians played *oudes* and wailed ancient desert songs of jubilation.

Page 37: For eight centuries, the Ansari family of Old Jerusalem has provided *khatteebs* (curators, or director-custodians) for the Dome of the Rock. For six hundred years they have guarded the original key to the mosque's main portal. An Ansari has served, and serves, in every important and also simple function in protecting the shrine, while also providing needed manpower to run its various services, including aid to pilgrims from the entire Moslem world.

Sheikh Mahmoud Ansari, 70, in charge of all cleaning of the mosque, would himself daily wash the stones between the marble columns of the pulpit built in the southern arcade in 1387, by Al-Malek az-Zaher Barqouq, an area reserved for the highest dignitaries during prayers. Directly beneath the *haram* of the mosque (the 34-acre compound surrounding the building itself) there are 27 cisterns which, when full after winter rains, hold ten million gallons of fresh water. There are no wells in Old Jerusalem. Thus the city, in periods of drought, became a vulnerable fortress during those long years when it lay under siege.

The northern arcade, opposite Sheikh Mahmoud, is called the Bab-al-Jannah. First mention of such a name originated with Jacob, who, legends say, spoke with God from the Rock and named it "The Gate to Paradise." For centuries, the Bab-al-Jannah has been a singularly sacred area in the already holy mosque, for it is there that most funeral processions halt for a moment, before climbing along the winding trail leading to the Moslem cemetery on the rocky slopes of the Mount of Olives.

Page 38: Moslem invaders under the Moorish Caliphs dominated Spain from the beginning of the eighth until the end of the fifteenth century, an almost endless era of clashing armies and anguish, but sometimes peaceful accomodation. The Alhambra of Granada, and the Great Mosque of Córdba, remain today as the westernmost symbols of the Bedouin warriors who swept up out of the Arabian peninsula to transform the character of much of the then-known world. The Alhambra, because of earlier neglect and sporadic—often lavish—additions, now probably bears little resemblance to the palace-filled fortress first commissioned by Mohammed ibn al-Ahmar in 1248, yet it is still a monumental reminder of Islam's earlier military power, and Spain's tormented past. And although altered today, the citadel offers a vivid portrait of the wealth and refinement and perhaps even the atmosphere of life within the palaces during those historic reigns, of those who ruled as near-dieties—far from austere Mecca.

The *Torre de las Damas* (Tower of Ladies), with its enormous reflection pool filled with shoals of undulating goldfish and framed by palm trees and cypress, must have epitomized the harsh differences between the lives of those first invading, leather-faced, Koran-inspired Arab cavalrymen, and the elegant *caballeros* with their silk-and-lace *señoras* who bowed to even more refined and magnificently costumed Spanish monarchs.

Page 39: Legends and romanticized contemporary events possibly inspired the now-forgotten artist who received the order to decorate an alcove ceiling of the Hall of Kings in the Alhambra. Painted on gold—the gold itself on leather—and totally realistic, the images reveal the hand of an artist who abandoned the restrictive tenents of Islam and approached the ceiling with a luminous pallet, and a romantic heart. *(Front endpaper, pages 26 & 43)*

Page 40: Stars and semicrescents form a galaxy unto themselves among the walls of tiles lining the alcove of the *Patio de los Arrayanes* (Courtyard of Myrtles) in the heart of the Alhambra.

Page 41: Patio de los Arrayanes: a sanctum of classical tranquility, where sculpted arcades, carved doors, wrough-iron grilles, latticed screens, tile-and-script walls . . . and silence, harmonize.

Page 42; top: One of the stone sculptures from the fountain in the *Patio de los Leones,* the centerpiece attraction of the palace-fortress. Folktales and fanciful theories abound regarding the origin of the lions but the truth is unknown—even Granada's famed fortunetelling gypsies can reveal nothing.

Page 42; bottom: Sculpture and Kufic script were wed, creating art on corridor walls. The text, for all of its calligraphic elegance, is not Koranic at all—as the Islamic novice might assume—but rather the self-serving autobiography of deeds and piety of a long-ignored resident caliph.

Page 43: Moorish Caliph painted on gold-on-leather. The Hall of Kings. *(Front endpaper A, page 26)*

Page 44: The *mihrab* (prayer niche) window of the Alhambra, overlooking the gardens from above *El Patio de los Leones;* called the *Mirador de Lindaraja* (Balcony of Lindaraja—a girl).

Page 45: The Ceiling of Kings. *(Front endpaper A)*

Pages 46 & 47: The Great Mosque of Córdoba, called *"La Mesquita"* by Spaniards, was begun in 786 and finally completed in 999. After the Moors were defeated and forced out of Spain, the mosque was converted into a Catholic church—in sheer size, said to be second only to St. Peter's in Rome. Unlike Hagia Sophia in Istanbul, which now is only a museum reflecting the collision of Moslem and Christian architecture, the Great Mosque of Córdoba is today an active Catholic church (which actually occupies only a fraction of the sprawling labyrinthine structure).

Forests of arches now shelter Crucifixions symbolic of another Faith, yet the multiple Moorish arcades, illuminated by golden Spanish sunlight, seem appropriate in this singular shrine.

Pages 48-49: No one knows, for sure, the ethnic origin of the Berber tribes who moved into the High Atlas Mountains of northern Morocco more than five thousand years ago. They speak their own Hemitic tongue, not the Semitic language of the lowland Arabs who flank their isolated peaks and barren plateaus, who view them as foreigners—which they are not. They were the first settlers to migrate westward, from some Aryan birthplace in the eastern Mediterranean crescent (centuries before Arabs roamed out of the Persian Gulf deserts), leaving Neolithic ancestors behind but bringing their fair skin (hidden under windburn and burnooses), often hazel-green eyes, sometimes red hair, and even freckles. They also brought an agrarian lifestyle, the shepherd's love of vast horizons, and stubborn pride. Tribal customs have apparently remained little changed since they arrived in northwest Africa.

Berbers scorn the plow while utilizing the hoe, both Neolithic inventions. The horse is to be ridden—if one can afford such luxury—but never forced to suffer the indignity of bending to man as a draft creature. Wheels are equally foreign to their culture, although itinerant potters from the southern Sahara are welcomed in Berber villages where they replace broken household utensils. Berber men are serene and open-spaces handsome; men of a distant gaze, at home while alone in the worst of mountain storms. Berber girls are frequently sensational beauties, by any standard; unveiled, laughing exponents of *haute couture* high above the clouds; girls who look at strangers—and the rest of the world—eye to eye.

Berber homes are astonishing affairs, architectural mirages of soaring cubes that climb into the mountain mists—perhaps the world's first skyscrapers—even while being integral units of fortress-villages, complexes designed exclusively of adobe bricks and walls—nothing but straw and mud.

Aït M'Semrir, mysterious behind birch trees and emerald fields of spring's first planting, is typical of most Berber villages sprinkled along the banks of the Upper Dadès River where it flows down from melting snow fields in the surrounding mountains. The Upper Dadès Valley has been the home of two neighboring tribes, the Aït Hadiddou and Aït Morrhad, since Berbers first discovered the High Atlas Mountains.

Page 50: Children of the Aït Morrhad tribe await their mother, at work in distant mountain valleys cutting brush for fuel to heat their home in winter. *(page 1)*

Page 51: Brothers and a little sister in Aït Attiq (Aït Hadiddou tribe: revealed by the black-and-white blanket stripes) sit in spring sunshine hoping a trout will swim by while their parents visit the *souk* (weekly market) in nearby Aït Tilmi. The boys' hair is in different styles since each was born under a different patron "saint," which determines many things in a Berber's life. After puberty, a boy is shaved and usually remains shaven-headed under his turban until the end of his life. Some tribesmen deviate slightly, permitting themselves bristly crew cuts, much like Marines and Japanese soldiers during the Second World War. Girls, except for tribal blankets, appear free to dress choosing any color, necklace, silver bracelet or hat they desire—which they do with gusto and devastating impact in those otherwise often bleak mountain valleys.

Pages 52-53: Zaïd and his pet lamb play among the headstones of the tiny shepherd's ancestors in the village cemetery of Aït M'Hand. The markers are simply flat rocks carried from nearby slopes. Death, among tribesmen of the Upper Dadès Valley, brings almost no attendant ceremony. Burial and placement of headstone are arranged within a few hours by men of the family or village—and that is all.

Pages 54-55: For a Berber, washing the burnoose is a rite never entrusted to women. It is the only garment he personally launders, using no soap, only water, and the tremendous power of his pile-driver feet. His wife, infant trussed to her back, washes the rest of the family clothes. This tribesman of Aït Tfeqirt (resembling to an astonishing degree Yul Brynner as the exuberant King of Siam) slowly turned, while grunting a hoarse songlike chant, as he drove his feet down into the soaking burnoose. The great flat rock upon which he appeared to dance was the traditional washing stone of his village.

Page 56: Women of the Aït Hadiddou tribe spend long hours spinning wool into yarn for their distinctive blankets and gathering backbreaking loads of brush in mountain valleys far from home. Their men plant and till the fields; others, especially the old and very young, are shepherds.

Page 57: Berbers, in earlier days, may have owned a few slaves from Black Africa, from the Sahara east of their mountains. Today, children of those servants still live among the Berbers as equal members of the tribe and village. This elegant lady, aristocrat in any society, sat against an old wall spinning woolen yarn, using Neolithic spindle and whorl. It was market day in Aït M'Semrir; most of her neighbors were seated nearby.

Almost all negotiations in a Berber *souk* are conducted by men who appear to have time for everything, particularly visiting with other men after a week of working their fields by hand. No tractor, no draft animal, no plow—working with only two hands. Women come to the *souk* to visit and act as hitching posts for the livestock offered for sale.

The Aït M'Semrir *souk* is almost a family affair, as it must have been for centuries, attracting old friends and neighbors from miles around. Almost every woman is costumed differently, although identifiable by tribal blanket. Except for turbans and color variations of the burnoose, a tribesman's clothing is similar to that worn by most men of North Africa and the Moslem Middle East. One characteristic of a Berber *souk* distinguishes it from those of the lowland neighboring Arabs: all Upper Dadès bargaining is nearly inaudible, with none of the good-natured but sometimes almost deafening haggling that often accompanies such dealings in markets of more distant lands. Typical of all, when closing a transaction the vendor shakes hands with the purchaser, then kisses the bundle of bank notes—sealing the sale.

Pages 58 & 59: Men of Aït M'Semrir relax in the sunshine of early spring before walking to the nearby *souk,* an open area adjacent to the village. All enfold themselves in burnooses of wondrously sun-faded or somber colors. No Renaissance painter could have chosen shades more subtle for Biblical themes—which appears relevant, since that was probably near the region where Berber garb and sensibilities were also born.

Pages 60-61: As they head for home, in the valley far below, brush cutters of Aït Tilmi cross a desolate plateau many miles from the mountainside where they already had worked for hours gathering winter fuel. There, they had tied counter-balancing stones to the windward side of their crushing loads—often weighing more than themselves—to prevent their being blown off course by the gales that often strike from clear skies in that treeless wilderness.

Pages 62-63: Aït M'Semrir, one of the great Berber fortress-villages, is flanked by stone corrals where the cows and mules of the more affluent families are kept. The owner of a horse generally tethers it apart. During winter, as customary in most alpine regions, all livestock is sheltered in the village's cavernous ground-floor stables for protection and to help heat the living quarters of families above.

Pages 64 & 65: Late spring afternoon high in the Upper Dadès Valley, as brush cutters of Aït Oussikis *(64)* and Aït Attiq *(65)* return home and men of the villages till their fields until dark.

Pages 66 & 67: Women of Aït Tfeqirt weave a burnoose on their loom—work taking about fifteen days—while husbands add precious brush sparingly to a fire on which to brew tea. The only light piercing the darkness comes from tiny vents in the ceiling and an occasional miniature window in the massive earthen walls. Like stone houses of mistral-buffeted Provençal France, where windows are almost nonexistent and the constant wind and searing heat of summer are viewed as natural enemies, Berber homes today still reflect Neolithic man's initial preoccupation with the elements and his determination to live better than when *his* ancestors hunkered down in primordial caves.

Daughters grind wheat between stones that had been used by generations of the family, as chickens wander through the gloom pecking for overlooked kernels. On Fridays, the loom is dismantled and removed completely from the room, honoring the Moslem Sabbath.

Page 68: Aïcha M'Bark, 16, of Aït Tfeqirt, pauses for a moment while grinding maize and barley, together with a sprinkling of rock salt, to provide flour for that day's family bread. Chin tatoos reveal her ancestry—the Aït Morrhad tribe—while the tiny Robin Hood-style cap and cheek-framing bangs make the ultimate statement of femininity and family honor—virginity.

Page 69: Old Moha Ou Youssef, not a Berber (as his features reveal), came from the southern Sahara, bringing his stone wheel of a potter, to mold and market his wares among villages where use of the wheel in any form or application had always been ignored. He later built a shed-home adjacent to but separate from the village complex of Aït Tfeqirt, where he had placed his gear while filling orders for replacements of broken crockery. The heavy wheel is turned by foot, each vessel shaped with fingers until the final moment when a smooth stone is pressed into the whirling clay to give it an even surface. New stock is replenished during the first days of every week, dried in direct sunlight for at least two days, then fired in the simple kiln behind his little home—which often nearly disappears under piles of the mountain brush needed to stoke his fire. By *souk* day he is ready.

Seated in darkness, clothed in a rough garment of Old Testament austerity, almost caressing the work coming to life under his fingers, and crowned with a golden-ivory turban, the Saharan Negro would have been immortalized had Rembrandt only discovered him in that remote Berber village of the Atlas Mountains.

Pages 70-71: The wife and field-stone home of Zaïd Abou Moha, in Aït Tilmi, create the impression of their having survived, untouched, since the age of Neolithic man. The house, pieced together without even adobe plastering in the niches of its herring-bone rock walls, was a masterwork revealing man's ability to adapt to his immediate environment—to create art from materials literally underfoot.

Pages 72 & 73: Berber girls of the Upper Dadès pursue their own tastes in fashion, alone. Handmade embroideries, silk-rope headbands, mammoth amber beads, glass beads, stone beads, random coins, the hand of Fatimah, hammered silver bracelets, tatoos, flashing eyes, homemade mascara of liquified local black lead, capes and cloaks and lost in day dreams, and sultry over-the-shoulder curiosity about a non-Berber nomad roaming the High Atlas Mountains . . . the Upper Dadès, on a good day, was very good, indeed.

Pages 74-75: The Tribunal of Elders of the Aït Hadiddou hear testimony during the trial of a shepherd and a grass girl, at Aït Tilmi. After weighing statements of other brush cutters (this photograph), major questions remained unresolved. Deliberations were suspended awaiting more evidence: adultery, or rape? Then the case would be submitted to Rabat, the seat of central government and justice for all of Morocco.

Pages 76-77: Idir, the shepherd, with his flock of sheep and goats high on a slope of the Atlas Mountains overlooking the Upper Dadès Valley. Huge flat stones lay strewn everywhere. His wards picked their way through them in search of grass, or moss, anything edible. The day had been overcast and sullen, perhaps much like it was when Stone Age children tended their flocks and guarded them from predators; responsible, too, for their families' fortunes since disaster would overwhelm them if anything should happen to the flock.

Pages 78-79: The shepherd and his son, and flock, arrive home at nightfall with the turret-towers of Aït M'Hand silhouetted against the sky.

Page 80: Five thousand years of freedom and pride, and dignity: the Matriarch of Aït M'Semrir.

Page 81: Among all of the tribes that roam across the Sahara Desert and other wastelands of North Africa, the veiled Blue Men—the Tuaregs—are perhaps the most dramatic in appearance. They are the caravaners who for centuries carried salt and cargo to oases outposts, the most famous—Timbuktu. Today, they still lead camel trains through the dunes and wind-scarred rocky plateaus where no others follow, and where few but Tuareg nomads have ever been. Today, too, these statuesque loners are among the last of the free, the wanderers in the world of Allah. Yet even they are being touched, if ever so lightly, by the impact of the post-war world on isolated cultures: tourists cling precariously to saddle horns and humps, as Tuareg caravans undulate toward the horizon.

The Tuareg tribes belong to a loosely organized desert brotherhood answering to the Amenokal of the Ahaggar Tuareg Confederation, who, when he can be found, is sometimes seen in Tamanrasset, in southern Algeria. The Amenokal—a kinglike title—is a towering, six foot three, two hundred fifty pound monolith of sheer gloom about whom little more has been recorded. The only person said to be capable of penetrating the regal shadows is his court jester, Baleyel (white cloaked), as in the Dark Ages.

Pages 82-83: European tourists traversing the Ahaggar Mountains in southern Algeria, enjoy the view from aboard (and behind) camels of a Tuareg caravan as it winds through some of the most spectacular scenery on earth . . . if one relates to horizons untouched by any hand but God's. For the novice caravaner, staying aloft astride a swaying and sometimes lurching camel as the earth passes far below, is perhaps comparable to the experiences of a novice astronaut, first time out from Cape Kennedy—locked into seemingly eternal weightless orbit.

Page 84: The caravan leader was Barka, a silent, cypress-tall, dreamy-eyed young Tuareg nobleman who had been veiled since puberty and would remain shielded from searching gaze until he died. When things went amiss for the tourists—the caravan had been chartered for a week by a travel company: inadequate camping gear, little water, improper food (dried spaghetti!)—Barka and his fellow Tuaregs could do nothing but express laconic regrets: no slaves had been signed on for the tourists, and it was beneath the social and tribal caste of the tribesmen to contribute their physical help. It was forbidden by their code: the Europeans became the forlorn Untouchables of the Sahara.

Page 85: Tambarek, the desert nightingale of Tamanrraset, plays her one-stringed *imzad* while humming balladlike songs of the Sahara. Unlike nobleman Barka, who had been veiled since youth, Tambarek—from one of the most lowly of Tuareg tribes—was never veiled and seemed, in many ways, freer of tribal restraints and ethics than any of the men. She cradled the *imzad* between hands with fingers that seemed to be extensions of the instrument itself. Her earrings tinkled and shone as she moved her head ever so slightly, a silver cascade of rings and beads and chains falling to her breast.

Notes on Libya predating the eminence of Colonel Muammar el-Qaddafi: or Trying to Understand in a Postcard Country Trying to Discover Itself. Or, The Road from Roman Ruins to Rommel's Wreckage is Worth Exploring.

In 1943, when the German armies were driven from Africa, the British became trustees and administrators of the northern Libyan desert regions—Cyrenaica in the east and Tripolitania in the west—under articles of the Hague Convention. France had moved into the mysterious, and rumored as possibly oil-rich, enormous southern region known as the Fezzan, which no foreigner (non-Frenchman) was known to have penetrated. Even by 1950, travel between Cairo and Tripoli along the single deeply rutted Mediterranean coast road was a spine-jolting experience—and equally shocking as a journey into human frustration.

The British, as the occupying power in Libya, seemed to have done everything in their power to promote differences between Cyrenaica and Tripolitania. Egyptian pounds were used as currency in Cyrenaica, only military script was legal tender in Tripolitania. The Cyrenaicans were granted "self government" under the British-subsidized Emir Idris Senussi, a semi-senile stooge who had initially received his title role from the Italians, when *they* were supporting him, after the First World War. Cyrenaica was also given a "Constitution" —written in London. The residents of Cyrenaica were mostly nomads, said to be 95 percent illiterate. One, one-page weekly newspaper had been promised for the following year.

In Tripolitania (10 percent nomadic, Italianized, literate) there was not a single newspaper or radio station owned and operated by Tripolitanians: there was one, one-page Arabic daily, and one, one-page Italian sheet, both published by the British Information Office, censured, employing no local reporters nor subscribing to any news service other than Reuters. Even though the Germans and Italians had been the enemy during the war, local Arabs now had to conform to the same regulations as any Italians remaining in the country. Public or private assembly was prohibited without written consent of the British Military Administration. When local politicians wanted to send delegates to the United Nations General Assembly in Lake Success, the British refused them the necessary dollars in exchange for their military script, over the sum total of $400, regardless of the number of delegates. Envoys were forced to risk arrest to represent themselves, buying dollars on the black market in Egypt.

Travel between the two territories of the same country was at a standstill. Frontier control points (at Adjedabia, Cyrenaica, and Misurata, Tripolitania) were 404 miles apart. Anyone caught in that forbidden buffer zone without written permission of the British Military Authority was subject to a fine of $650 and a stiff jail term. Money from the salvage of war debris, both in the desert and from the various harbors, went into the British Treasury; none stayed in either territory. In the years immediately following the retreat of the Germans, prisoners of war were used to clear mines and to gather British dead from the still extremely dangerous desert. When the last POWs were sent home, all collecting ceased, although soldiers and mines remained scattered through the interior of the country, where shepherds and nomads continued to step on the explosives. When the British re-established Idris Senussi as Emir, they gave him an annual salary equal to that of the President of the United States, with an additional $15,000 for "expenses," and another $90,000 for "repatriation of relatives" (most lived in Alexandria, Egypt, one day by road, or a couple of air-hours away; for whom $63,000 had been allotted the year before for the same reason). Those outlays, in addition to the total cost of administrating the Cyrenaican territory (Tripolitania took one-third as much) cost the British Treasury about $4,500,000—a bargain, when one realized that the idea behind the dream was to replace war-lost bases in Greece, Egypt and Palestine. And who knew what truth might exist in ever-more exciting reports of secret explorations revealing the presence of the finest grade oil waiting to be tapped under those endless stretches of enigmatic Libyan sands?

Many fires forge character in a nation and its people. Libya's long history of invaders and occupation is one that few countries can match. Famed conquerors attempted subjugation or colonization—Athens, Rome, Constantinople—of that strategically alluring but hostile portion of the North African coast which extends southward across plateaus and deserts to encompass a land mass one-sixth larger than Alaska, itself once viewed as a worthless wilderness. Without exception, each invader lost far more than his impeccably crafted armor or shirt. Hitler and Mussolini were only the most recent. No one can calculate the blood and treasure that have disappeared into that historically trampled sand. Even Britain, arriving as a well-supported victor, attempted to stay with a veiled policy of aloof detachment while investing just enough to ensure political control: should the tide turn, move on.

The tide *has* now turned—oil, supreme light crude, full flood—with surf crashing upon beaches where the deep footprints of marauders may soon be swept away.

Finally, the people and the land itself . . . so vast, so desolate; always before viewed as abandoned by Allah . . . as destitute of resources and dreams as any fragment of forgotten earth on Earth: an acrid oasis nourished only by the bitter wells of hopelessness. A few herdsmen and desert wanderers, illiterate, of course, like all of their ancestors, who, in their lifetimes, had heard of only one Book . . . which they knew by heart.

Page 86: Leptis Magna, between Benghazi and Tripoli, was the jewel among Roman North African colonies that flourished on Mediterranean shores during the First Century A.D. Mussolini's government spent vast sums in excavating the site, restoring the Forum and theater, and the classical market place, as evidence of Italy's historic right to the territory. Even today, breathtaking monuments survive to substantiate the claim that Leptis Magna is one of the greatest, and most dramatic, archaeological wonders of the world. Here, the towering battered head of Medusa stares out across the ruins toward the Basilica and Forum . . . and seemingly at the tragedies that have been played out, center stage, during Libya's past.

Page 87: Just one of the forests of crosses standing in stark silhouette against the cloudless Libyan sky. Maltese crosses, Catholic crosses, ordinary Christians' crosses, Protestant British headstones, Stars of David, Moslem Crescents and Stars—and unmarked sagging rectangles in the once-unturned desert crust.

Page 88-89: All manner of war equipment lined the road between Tobruk and Derna for many years after the Second World War. Tanks, trucks, even an enormous Italian field gun, which became home-of-the-day for goats of Bedouin shepherds sitting on a treeless knoll nearby.

Page 90: Bedouin shepherds seemed indifferent to the blatant charms of "The Venus of Garien," an exuberant nude-map-mural of North Africa painted on an abandoned Italian garrison wall in the Libyan countryside, seventy-five miles south of Tripoli. British and Australian soldiers depicted, are engaged in campaigns on terrain not usually associated with warfare in the desert. The ever-present word "wadi" is Arabic for oasis. Clifford Saber, American Field Service, signed and dated his masterpiece . . . A.D. 1943.

Page 91: Another artist carved Caesar's immortal name into the limestone flank of a long-dry aqueduct at Leptis Magna . . . A.D. 43; not the first of the graffiti in the Libyan desert, where prehistoric man left painted diaries of his hunts on sacred rocks deep in the Sahara.

Pages 94-95: Bedouin *hadjis*—pilgrims—meet beneath the silhouette of a once lethal German gun, after completing the trip to Mecca.

Pages 94-95: A Tripolitanean child-shepherd with his pet lamb, at dawn, awaits the first shower of the winter rainy season that will bring grass.

Page 96: Gazala and Karieh watched without blinking when a stranger found them on a street corner in Tripoli. Young ladies who asked for nothing more than rewarded curiosity.

Page 97: The forced abdication of Egypt's King Farouk in 1952, raised two immediate questions in the Nile Valley: the nature of his young army officer revolutionary successors, and the nature of the treasures rumored to be hidden in special strongrooms of his Cairo and Alexandria palaces. Colonel Gamal Abdel Nasser and his colleagues soon answered the first question, and thanks to him cameras were in the palaces during that initial stunned survey, when no one knew what the next room or sealed vault—guarded by infrared scanners that locked into networks of other alarms—would reveal. Weeks passed; more hidden chambers were unearthed. Priceless treasures lay next to porno trash.

One of the world's finest collections of rare stamps was cataloged with another of coins dating to Hellenistic mints, so refined that few but the greatest museums—or a king—could have acquired it. There were heirloom Turkish carpets from his dynasty's ancestors' palaces, rooms filled with French furniture from other kings' collections, trays of gems racked upon other trays of gems bought with an expert's eye from networks of dealers worldwide and which only Farouk and his private art sleuths had ever gloated over together—the young monarch was as secretive as he was schizophrenic, obese, intelligent, and surely tormented. For, in adjacent—sometimes the same—fanatically guarded vaults, inventory-taking officers were shocked, and acutely embarrassed (with a foreigner present), to discover their ex-Majesty's collection of pornographic pulp magazines, paintings, stimulants, photographs, and even statues, stacked, crated, hung on walls, stashed in corners, and indexed with the same affection and concern for security as had been lavished on the gold-and-diamonds coffee service wedding present from his Parliament, and the golden Pharaonic funeral mask that he had "borrowed" from the Egyptian Antiquities Museum.

Page 98 & 99: Few but royalty ever walked the corridor in Ras el Tin Palace, Alexandria, that joined the Queen's and King's bedrooms. Her private chambers—forbidden even to male members of the family—were called the *salamlek*, the ladies' isolated living quarters. The bedroom of the last Queen of Egypt.

Page 100: Kubbah Palace, Cairo *(upper left)*; Farouk's fantasies *(upper center)*; Montazah Palace, Alexandria *(upper right)*; Ras el Tin Palace *(bottom)*. Kubbah was the principal residential palace of Farouk when living in Cairo during winters. In summer, he and his family alternated between Montazah and Ras el Tin. Both were on the Mediterranean, with a yacht at Ras el Tin, beaches at Montazah. Abdin Palace, in Cairo, held a Throne Room—another was in Ras el Tin—and official offices.

Page 101: The Summer Throne of the last King of Egypt, Ras el Tin Palace, Alexandria. A magnificent Turkish eighteenth-century Ghiordes prayer rug seemed to dominate even the throne and the gilt-and-inlay walls of the classically Oriental chamber. Only this room and the Byzantine Room in Abdin Palace *(following pages)* fulfilled expectations of a Westerner who had tried to imagine the life of an Eastern potentate.

Pages 102-103: The Byzantine Room, Abdin Palace, Cairo. Golden mosaics of dancing girls, harps, a marble central fountain, and cushioned alcoves seen through the luminous sensuous glow of dimmed chandeliers.

Page 104: The last whirling dervish in Egypt, Mohammed el Attar, "about seventy," danced one morning beneath minarets of Cairo's Sultan Hassan and Sultan Ahmed mosques. All other members of his cult had disappeared from Egypt (where they had been banned by King Farouk's father, Fuad), with most of them probably returning to Turkey where they had originated, near Konya, in the eleventh century. Fighting a strong cross wind, the old exorcist spun tirelessly—a purist, a frustrated artist striving for perfection as gusts kept deflating his skirt which ideally should have arced straight away from his waist: the falcon in diving flight. His felt cap was a *caouk* (Turkish—not Arabic). After spinning for about an hour he abruptly stopped —without the slightest evidence of disturbed equilibrium—excused the malfunctions of his skirt, then excused himself once again to return to dancing, saying he was out of practice—he would like to whirl a bit more, maybe for the rest of the day.

Page 105: Zar dancers from the Upper Sudan, in Cairo. *(pages 4-5)*

Page 106: In Islam, the three days following Ramadan—the holy month commemorating Mohammed's receiving the Message of the Koran—are Bairam, which themselves celebrate the end of Ramadan. In Cairo, it is a joyous occasion marked by feasts, boat rides on the Nile and visits to relatives—and to the graves of ancestors in the City of the Dead which sprawls almost endlessly above the Old City. Only the vast, sculpture-encircled tombs of ancient Chinese emperors, and the rolling acres of headstones and mausoleums that carpet entire suburbs around New York, can equal in size the stark sun-drenched necropolis that is a sanctuary of silence for mourning families who often bring picnics while escaping the bedlam and crush of Old Cairo during those first days after Ramadan. One black-scarfed, amber-necklaced, classically profiled teen-age widow seemed to embody every proud memory, and lonely tear there.

Page 107: A Pepsi vendor's midday prayers to Mecca, from Cairo's Nile bridge, join those of millions of other Moslems who have stopped whatever they may have been doing, at the same time, to worship: no cathedral, temple or monastery; no priest, rabbi, minister or monk; no pageant, sermon, chant, costume, candle or hymn; no donation or solicitation; no picnic, party, dance or bingo; no image—benign, bereaved or crucified; no ordained saint or confirmed miracle; no literature but one Book . . . and no god but Allah.

Pages 108 & 109: Ramadan in Old Cairo is celebrated today as it has been for centuries. Daytime pyramids of fruit await nightime cannons that break the fast. Children clutch copper piastres for the old lamp maker who has always lived in the wall of the bazaar. A woman awaiting dawn prayers of Bairam appears to be etched into the *khemsa* (gaudily painted tarpaulins used for mass prayers, great weddings and State funerals) covering Republic Square—a raven in the Garden of Allah. Her silhouette mirrors the midnight-black *mihrab* behind the golden pillars of the Turkish eighteenth-century Ladiq prayer rug, treasured as one of the masterpieces in Cairo's Museum of Islamic Art.

Pages 110 & 111: Four ancient cannons, firing a 21-gun barrage, signal the end of Ramadan and the beginning of Bairam, the three-day period of jubilation—Christmas and New Year's Eve combined. Even as the blasts echoed through the Old City that sprawls around the base of the Citadel and Mohammed Ali Mosque, families broke fasts, lights twinkled atop minarets *(frontispage)*, and millions of residents celebrated the start of a new year; a different time every Bairam because of the Islamic lunar calendar. Before dawn, tens of thousands of men had left their neighborhoods and headed for Republic Square (which commemorates Nasser's revolution) to gather for prayers in front of Abdin Palace, where recently towered the Winter Throne of the Playboy King of the Nile—where tourists now pay a few piastres to make Polaroid shots of the last monuments of the last dynasty of a country of dynasties of Pharaohs who built a world so lavish within our world it has never been rivalled, but which has now ended on Farouk's own prophecy . . .

"Tomorrow, there will be only five Kings—of England, and in a deck of cards."

Pages 112-113: Women of Old Cairo, Ramadan ended and prayers of Bairam finished, sit in silence for a moment before returning home. *(page 109, back endpaper B)*

Notes on Gaza Strip predating the eminence of Yasser Arafat and of Menachem Begin: or Trying to Understand in the Land of the Bible—Torah—Koran. Or, the Gaza—Beersheba Road is Strewn with More than Memories of Wrecked Temples and Ruined Dreams.

Pages 114 through 134: It was an old, old land—old when Samson destroyed the Temple, they say right in Gaza Town, across Main Street, where the rich man's Cadillac now parks amid the clutter and confusion and contrast of two hundred thousand desperately poor displaced people trying to find the answer to survival. There is no resentment—the man is building the largest clinic in town. It was an ancient land when nearby Neolithic Man tamed the fields and the grain plants of the meadows, and began sifting kernels from chaff—just as gnarl-fingered, gold-turbaned patriarchs still work for their daily bread. Their sons threshed in fields beside them, running snowy donkeys in tight circles, freeing kernel from husk—the thread of the future woven into their young bodies, and into the unknown fabric of their tomorrows in this homeland of Hebrew-Christian-Moslem men. *(page 27)*

It is a land of peasant farmer and Bedouin shepherd, where changes came slowly, or not at all, even though it cradled some of the more majestic minds that have moved our world. Grapes . . . grain . . . oranges, famed throughout the Bible Land, these and a few other crops grew well in the northern pockets of rich dark earth that had been cultivated since before recorded time, but in the desert south fertile soil was as rare as the rain that almost never fell. Now, multitudes of homeless families have become trapped on those straining fields—refugees from the northern valleys and nearby rocky hills that had always been home, however bountiful or bleak, since bearded father and threshing sons first worked harvests from their bit of earth.

Shimmering mists rising with the dawn . . . slowly arching combers curving toward horizons far beyond any man's vision . . . tumbled dunes swelling and falling until lost among those veils shielding another day. This is the Sea . . . the Sea of Phoenician and Homer and Saint Paul, and of the sardine fishermen of Gaza today. Surely, if this shore is the Holy Land, this is the Holy Sea. Rythmic . . . serene . . . benevolent, wedded as no other to men who have launched their boats every night of every year of every century of every generation of all the fishermen on her shore. Before any word was written, she loved and embraced and protected and fed her men and their families. Should any sea on Earth rightfully be called His Sea, it is here—shining in the light of morning.

Sunrise glittering beneath his lids—a scar-faced askari from the Sudan . . . soundless . . . fighting camels from the Sahara padding that Mediterranean shore . . . coin-rimmed faces . . . flame-and-black veils . . . tatooed wrists—Bedouin shepherds' women drifting silently behind their flocks . . . netmen of a thousand-thousand voyages repairing torn meshes while awaiting another night on their sea—the shore, here, a slender thrust of naked desert and rocky plateau . . . a single road that was a path that was a legend over which have passed Allied half-tracks and a British half-man half-myth and Turkish cavalrymen and Arab and Roman and Greek and Persian conquerors, and others, and the Holy Family, and, truly, only God knows who—for this is southern Palestine; again a tortured-tranquil paradoxical place where the population has forever seemed to ebb and then flood with fleeing families, and where, now, Arabs and Israelis fight and falter and live and perish and try, each of them, to find the road to personal salvation.

And yet, in the end, more than a land, more than a sea, this pageant place called Gaza Strip is a pathetic pen for people . . . people who fled, as they always have from fire and fear, when artillery shells and bombs shattered their villages and means of life—crushed them so completely that today hundreds of thousands of refugees still cling precariously to the edges of fields that were barren before they arrived . . . where they now wait . . . without homes . . . without work . . . generally without hope . . . few without anger—none without black frustration and shame, looking at himself living on charity on the border of his homeland . . . living where wheat and milk and meat and salt and sugar, and everything is rationed and nothing wasted—nothing, that is, but life itself.

If this country has a soul, it must be about crushed by the perpetual load of heartbreak it has borne.

Page 135: Asia and Europe meet at the Bosphorus Straits, where in winter handline fishermen brave the blizzards that sweep across the Black Sea from the Russian steppes beyond. Aegean—Dardanelles—Marmara—Bosphorus—Black Sea . . . the all-weather channel, ever-nagging dream of each ruler of every Kremlin dynasty. Seen through driven flakes that veil the minarets and ships and Golden Horn of Istanbul, the Asiatic western edge of Turkey seems unrelated to any dream of any conqueror, yet some of the most illustrious Western generals and now-legendary Eastern chieftans clashed and crossed, and won fame here.

Pages 136-139: Atop a fortress hilltop in Kars, on the Soviet frontier of Turkey, an emerald-green cloth is always draped over the rough stone coffin of Djelal Baba, "Daddy Djelal," a hero whose name symbolizes his country's sword-hewn respect for a fighting man. Papa Baba deserves a shrine: he died in 1239 battling the Horde of Genghis Khan, but only after ignoring "no less than seventy wounds." His well-attended and reportedly rather lavish mausoleum was destroyed by Russian invaders in the War of 1877, and destitute admirers were reluctant to rebuild, unsure what the future might bring. They had cause for restraint. Eastern Turkey, around Kars—almost under the long shadow of Mount Arat where Noah's Ark found port after the Flood—is not a place where foreigners or civic planners have been viewed with much enthusiasm. For good reason. The ancestors of local residents had watched almost endless columns of ravaging visitors arrive.

To date: Kumans (Kipchaks)—1064-1068; Georgians—1153; Mongols—1239; Persians—1502; Persians—1548; Russians—1828; Russians—1856; Russians—1870 (attack failed); Russians—1877; Russians—1878 (Kars ceded to Moscow under Treaty of St. Stefan); 1918—Kars returned to Turkey under Treaty of Brest-Litovich, at the end of the First World War. Sultans defeated; Ottoman Empire dismembered; Allied occupying forces withdrawn; Armenians and Greeks purged; Republic founded under Ataturk. Invasions ceased.

Brigadier General Avni Mizrak, commanding Turkey's always alerted, any-terrain, all-expert cavalrymen, was hated by the Russians for his role in the First World War. He apparently put the fear of Allah in the hearts of even Cossacks, who called him "Kara Avni Begov" . . . "Count Black Avni." Astride barrel-chested, dapple gray Toros, named for bastion mountains in the south, Black Avni—hand thrust into the winter sky—seemed to challenge the future, the only enemy that could defeat him, turning his snow-flecked squadrons into images of the past.

Pages 140 through 157: The late Shah of Iran, as his father had before him, attempted to prohibit the annual migration of the great nomadic tribes across southern deserts into the central mountains of the

270

country, following trails worn smooth by their ancestors when the land was still Persia. Then, the rythm of slowly advancing and receding flocks, moving with the seasons, was viewed as part of nature, ordained by Allah, just as were the arrival of winter's first snow and summer's rose, and the changes of the moon and positions of the stars—the visible pulse of life itself. The Shahs' view was that nomadic migration was an anachronism reflecting decadence in Iranian character—a flawed facet in the jewel being polished by Tehran, a society that would achieve a brilliance compatible with the Court of the Peacock Throne itself.

Both shahs are now gone and today another extremist in Tehran issues fanatical one-man decrees through spokesmen of his religious court—tracts preoccupied with self-judged decadence among his Moslem neighbors, threats of Israel, and hatred for the Great Satan, America—leaving the nomads in peace . . . migrating as they have since the promise of grass first lured them out of their Persian Gulf deserts, to meadows above Isfahan.

The Qashqai (gosh-guy) tribes possess ancestral title to, and migrate through, approximately 32,000 square miles of southern and central Iran, and control—by their presence—another 50,000 square miles of bordering deserts, mountains and meadows along their paths. They follow the new grass of spring, as every generation of their grandfathers did as far back as their oral history extends—which carries them back, first, to the mountains of Azerbaidjan, three hundred years ago, then, before that, into the steppes of some remote corner of eastern Turkestan where tribal lore claims they originated as the cavalrymen whose families tended flocks for Genghis Khan.

Qashqai tribesmen view city-born Iranians with aloof detachment (until they disrupt the tempo of their lives), bemused contempt (when Koran-quoting extremists belabor occasional visitors to Isfahan with urban experts' views of Allah) and, always, as possible foes. The nomads speak a Turkoman dialect, not Iranian Farsi, unless faced by cityfolk or government agents who periodically appear, threatening to organize their lives. They pay their taxes in sheep and goats (3 percent of the flock) to their khans, and leave to them the problems of dealing with Tehran—considered a bargain—while they return to their flocks, where they await the next migration.

While Qashqai is the name of the entire tribe, its population includes forty-four subtribes of which only four are considered significant: Ameleh, Dareh Shoori, Kashkuli, and Sheshboluki. Each has its own khans, or ruling family, its own route of migration, and its own assigned pasturage in both summer and winter quarters. Over each of the tribes and subtribes stands the Qashqai family.

After the death of the Khan of Khans in a prison of Shah Reza Pahlavi (who had founded his "King of Kings" dynasty, in 1925) during the Second World War, the Qashqai empire was ruled by four khans— brothers—and their mother. The new Khan of Khans, Mohammed Nasser Qashqai, the eldest brother, was the strongman not only of the tribe but of all southern Iran (which the Qashqais always referred to as Persia). The next two brothers, Malik Mansur and Mohammed Hosein, were Oxford graduates who spoke fluent English. Malik Mansur lived permanently with the tribe, while Mohammed Hosein spent much of his time in Tehran where he represented tribal interests concerning the government. Khosro, the youngest khan, had never been outside Iran, where he enjoyed the reputation of being the toughest, wildest fighter of all tribesmen; on two occasions he routed government forces sent to subdue the Qashqai. In the mountains during migration, there was rarely a night when he neglected diagramming ambushes throughout the entire tribal domain, to be activated should the Shah's troops ever again try to breach his stronghold.

Above all of her sons loomed the slender, usually silent, black-swathed figure of the Khan Mother, Khardijeh, who, many believed, was the final arbiter in all major questions of intratribal character. It was she, they said, who was the binding force that kept the Qashqai nomads so closely knit; the tribe that was "The Tribe," when outsiders spoke in awe of the myriad galloping horsemen who had appeared overnight, silhouetted on distant ridges—only to vanish, during migration. It was she who snuggled down into the piled cushions and carpets in her favorite corner of the great *majlis* tent (the Khan of Khans' colossal black goat-hair tent where he welcomed all Qashqai tribesmen and passing horsemen-neighbors) while watching her sons, at dusk, casually spinning and turning, firing army rifles apparently without sighting, to drop skittering swallows from the darkening sky, as shouting tribesmen snatched off winged felt caps and raced each other, arms outstretched to catch them. And it was "Bibi," Khardijeh, the Khan Mother, who ordered the Khan of Khans, to take the family prayer rug from his tent to the horse waiting for a nomad who had finished their migration and now had to leave the mountains, saying goodbye—which became forever.

Pages 158 through 177: Among adventurers of the mid-twentieth century, two fantasies evoked instant images of romantic challenge and forbidden frontiers, of fossilized societies still locked in the bedrock of medieval time—lands so remote and shielded by nature that only a handful of lucky (or more resolute) explorers had ever reached their hearts. One was Lhasa, in Himalayan Tibet, which today is possibly even more inaccessible than before although somewhat less provocative, since the rape of country and culture sullied the allure of God's Kingdom in the Clouds—with roof-of-the-world temples now pillaged by Chinese soldiers, an aging Dalai Lama now in self-imposed exile, the theocratic legacy of her monks now in tatters and the rest of the world still indifferent.

The other goal of idealizing dreamers was Riyadh, the cubist-fortress, mud-brick capital of Saudi Arabia—rumored to loom sinister and impregnable whenever it did materialize from behind its guardian shield of blistering heat and blinding sandstorms . . . *shamals*, winds so fiendish, debilitating, constant and erosive, sentinel landmarks (marking distances between survival and starvation) were obliterated, familiar dunes vanished, unguarded wells were chocked within minutes and even small oases withered overnight. Few misconceptions enamored Riyadh to the wanderer—the place was no exotic vale from *The Thousand and One Nights* . . . no Sheherazade, with Harun al-Rashid lolling around on silken Persian pillows while fiddling with the fates of dancing girls and everyone else in his court. There was nothing—at that time—very dreamy about Saudi Arabia, or Riyadh—no resources, not even adequate drinking water—absolutely nothing at all. Except getting there, with the hope of meeting the king . . . if one dreamed about photographing the last great desert chieftan of nomadic tribesmen, a man who spoke in soft monosyllables, but each word counted, and was honored; an almost gentle giant of a man, half-blind and limping from ancient wounds, who still welcomed his Bedouin subjects as equals: the last warrior on horseback to create a kingdom then name it after his family. To his nomads, and almost every other Moslem on earth—Abdul Aziz. To the rest of the world—Abdul Aziz ibn Saud . . . Ibn Saud of Saudi Arabia. The title of "King" seemed almost superfluous. Just being the man was enough.

Another nomad, with a camera, met him for the first time at Dhahran, on the Persian Gulf, when he came down from his still-forbidden-without-royal-invitation palace in Riyadh, to visit the mysterious new world of the Arabian-American Oil Company that already was changing traditional life in the desert—probing under the sand, where they soon were to tap treasures in such profusion, and release a genie of such gigantic proportions, as to eclipse anything ever imagined in even the most exaggerated tales of Ali Baba—or Midas.

Hospitality and the exchange of gifts were traditions built into Bedouin etiquette, the ruling code of the desert after the holy Koranic laws themselves. When Ibn Saud visited Dhahran to tour Aramco's rapidly expanding installations, he sat beneath a gigantic palm tree-and-swords symbol of his reign (the handiwork of an amateur artist-driller from Texas) with an interpreter for the oil men at his feet. Many old cronies from their peninsula-conquering campaigns had arrived to greet him and sit in silence when others spoke of places and men and enemies that now meant nothing to anyone else, of the time when they were little more than desert-wise, guerrilla-war-veteran teen-agers, when Allah, for no understandable reason, chose them to be the ones to survive.

Other dignitaries seemed to be of another caste, not deep-desert born. The Sheikh of Kuwait resembled one of the Wise Men who followed the Star as they bore gifts to Bethlehem. *(page 159)* The Sheikh of Bahrain, a gnome nearly lost in lavishly embroidered cashmere *keffie* (head scarf) and camels hair *abba* (robe) trimmed with gold, was the nearest "foreigner" as a chief of state to attend. At that time, few outside the Persian Gulf knew, or cared very much, where Kuwait, Bahrain, Qatar, and those other pinpricks on the map of obscurity were. "State visits" were closed-circuit, regional and cozy, almost family affairs.

The Sheikh of Bahrain brought with him a bargeload of bitterly protesting gifts—forty camels: already ship weary, over-heated, sling-sore (belly straps had hoisted them ashore), and bored. They were still in Dammam, the then micro-port for Dhahran where all commerce was handled for Bahrain Island; on days without a *shamal*, clearly visible out in the Gulf. The camels never left the dock. After being admired and accepted in the King's name, they were slung back into their old berths on the barge, for the voyage back to Bahrain, and home—gifts to the Sheikh of Bahrain from the King of Saudi Arabia, in appreciation of the warmth of his welcome at Dhahran. The camels—permanent sling scars marking their chests—had never done anything else in their lives but serve as ambassadors of good will, making countless highest-priority voyages up and down the Persian Gulf—not a bad life, compared to plodding in caravans across the Great Arabian Desert.

Ibn Saud invited King Abdullah of Jordan to visit Riyadh as an act of reconciliation, to end more than thirty years of political feuding. Abdullah, a direct descendant of the Prophet, met Ibn Saud, the Guardian of Mecca, when the Royal Jordanian Air Force flagship (a war surplus U.S. Army DC-3) rolled to a stop alongside the black goat-hair Bedouin tent pitched at the edge of Riyadh's Royal Airport—a level stretch of wind-swept desert. Hoarse shouts of welcome arose from thousands of watching tribesmen when Abdul Aziz clamped his massive hand around Abdullah's slender fingers to escort him from the tent into the vintage (1920s), Bedouin-chauffeured, open Rolls Royce waiting to carry them to the turreted adobe Royal Palace in town, where the traditional Moslem three days of festivities celebrating an honored guest would begin.

They walked slowly, side by side; Abdullah diminutive but resplendent in pure white *abba*, embroidered gold-and-silk turban, a golden dagger glittering in his sash: massive Ibn Saud, wearing a Bedouin's red-and-white checkered *keffie*, his old-fashioned spectacles, comfortable palace slippers, and *carrying* his cane. For an instant, when they were seen together, one of the last pageant pages in mankind's history lay open—Macedonian generals . . . Incan emperors . . . Mongol khans . . . Knights of the Round Table . . . Persian poets . . . and the first shepherd kings—only to close again the moment they had passed.

King Abdullah was assassinated in Old Jerusalem—in the shadow of the Dome of the Rock—three years after his journey to Riyadh. Ibn Saud was to die only two years later . . . quietly; being graced, one hoped, with an old warrior's honorably earned peaceful eternity. Few men have left a more astonishing legacy: the Kingdom of Saudi Arabia, and more than thirty sons to shepherd it into the future.

Pages 178 through 185: Deep in the forests of East Africa skirting Lake Victoria, along lonely trails among endless tracts of trees and across mountain plateaus, often silently watched by herds of antelope, gazelle, elephant, or, sometimes, a leopard or dreaded Cape buffalo . . . in burning Equatorial sunlight, then drenched by rain-forest cloudbursts—through and around it all—rides a white-turbaned, sturdy little man on his bicycle. A tan briefcase dangles from the handlebars. A neat bundle of books bounces atop the rear wheel. Generally, the turbaned traveller is singing softly to himself—not popular tunes, but Moslem prayers. He is Hakeem Mohammed Ibrihim, physician, teacher, and the Ahmadiyya missionary for Uganda. *(pages 181-185)*

Mohammed Ibrihim was born in Pakistan, thirty-two years before arriving in Kampala. The son of a physician and landowner, he, too, was educated as a physician but of family lands he inherited nothing—all were lost during the British partition of India, in 1947. He was retrained as a missionary for African service, at the Ahmadiyya headquarters near Rabwah, Pakistan. He rarely finds time to practice as a physician, for his territory is all of Uganda, both north and south of the Equator, from Kenya to the Congo. To cover this country he travels more than three thousand miles each year on his bicycle, although sometimes friends going his way share their pickups—his bike tied atop their loads.

Unlike the other Ahmadiyya missionaries in Nairobi, or over in Lagos, he works by himself, without printing press or central office. Those other missions are chronically without sufficient funds with which to support their efforts but they are millionaires when compared to Hakeem (which means physician) Mohammed Ibrihim, who has absolutely nothing but his bicycle, books and literature—and his Faith. He also has a wife and several children, who live in a tiny earthern-floored house on the outskirts of Kampala, whom he rarely sees. He is constantly in the back country trying to spread the word of a religion in which he believes.

Hakeem Ibrihim—like most Ahmadiyya missionaries—makes no claim of having converted masses of Africans to Islam. For one period, between April and October of a "good year," he made but thirty-five conversions

—fully recognized converts accepted by his headquarters in Pakistan. However, he feels that he *has* managed to carry the word of Islam into places where it was never really known, nor understood before. He believes that the time is not too distant when many Africans will turn to Islam for answers to their spiritual and social needs. He thinks his present efforts will help them the day they might wish to turn to him, or to the man who follows him.

Hakeem Ibrihim feels sure that Africans are coming to the realization that Islam, more than Christianity or paganism, welcomes and recognizes each man as an equal—not subject to a witch doctor's caprice or the white man's segregation. He is also convinced that Islam is the only social force that might bring peace and tranquility to Africa, rent as it has been since mid-century by Mau Mau violence, apartheid, and anti-colonial, pro-communist, semi-literate, rampaging ultranationalism. But, most of all he feels that he is subject to Allah's will. In the early days, when he first arrived in Uganda, he was pelted with sticks and struck by stones, thrown by both pagans and Christians who were vehemently opposed to his missionary efforts in their areas. He told them that such violence was their privilege, and, in some cases, perhaps even their duty as they saw it—but that it also was his duty to come among them without protection, since fighting was not his business. He survived and now travels, freely, throughout even the most remote corners of Uganda.

Conversion to Islam by an Ahmadiyya missionary, following multiple meetings and lengthy instructions, takes place only after the fulfillment of specific requirements: (a); The applicant has been circumcised. (b); The Hakeem has preached the beauties of Islam, but only after the applicant has washed face, hands, and feet prior to attending the conversion ceremony. (c); There has been a question and answer period, all related to the Koran and Mohammed's teachings. (d); The applicant understands and agrees to the Ten Conditions of Islam as taught by the Ahmadiyyas. (e); The applicant signs the conversion papers (to be sent to and recorded at the Ahmadiyya Mission headquarters, Rabwah, Pakistan). (f); The applicant's name is changed to a Moslem name. (g); The applicant and the Hakeem pray together. (h); The final ceremonial and instructional ablutions are administered—called the *wazu*, in Arabic.

There are no other Moslem missionaries in Uganda, although the Ismailis have a semi-welfare society which is a civic group working on a limited scale in East Africa. The more orthodox Sunnis and Shi'ites do nothing related to missionary work. In fact, passionate feelings have been aroused among Sunnis and Shi'ites against the Ahmadiyyas, who, they believe, are preaching a new, streamlined Islam unrelated to the Koran. The Ahmadiyyas believe just the opposite, convinced that their understanding of Islam will keep Moslems abreast the times in an ever-changing world around them.

Conditions of Ba'ait (Allegiance) Laid Down by the Promised Messiah and Mahdi.
The Creed of the Ahmadiyya Sect, and the Oath (Ten Conditions) that every convert must swear to honor:

FIRSTLY, that up to the day of his death he shall abstain from worshipping any god but Allah.

SECONDLY, that he shall foreswear falsehood, adultry, gazing at women other than near relatives, cruelty, dishonesty, riot, rebellion and, in short, any kind of evil; and he shall not allow himself to be carried away by his passions, however strong they may be.

THIRDLY, that he shall say the five daily prayers without fail, according to the command of Allah and His Prophet; and to the best of his ability, he shall try to offer *Tahajjud* (night prayers), to invoke the blessings of Allah upon the Holy Prophet, to ask forgiveness for his own sins and pray for Allah's help and that, remembering Allah's blessings, he shall always praise Him.

FOURTHLY, that he shall in no way harm Allah's creatures in general and Moslems in particular by giving way to his passions—neither with the hand nor tongue nor any other means.

FIFTHLY, that in every state of pleasure or sorrow, prosperity or adversity, he shall prove himself faithful to Allah and that in every condition he shall submit to His Will, being ready to bear every kind of insult or pain; and in the hour of misfortune, he shall not turn away from Him but rather shall draw closer.

SIXTHLY, that he shall not follow vulgar customs and shall guard against evil inclinations and shall submit himself completely to the authority of the Holy Koran and make the Word of Allah and the sayings of His Prophet the guiding principles of his life.

SEVENTHLY, that he shall forsake pride and haughtiness and shall pass his days in humility, reserve, courtesy and meekness.

EIGHTHLY, that he shall consider his religion and the dignity and welfare of Islam dearer than his life, wealth and children and, in short, dearer than anything else.

NINTHLY, that he shall for the sake of Allah shows sympathy towards Allah's creatures and, to the best of his ability, he shall use his natural gifts for their welfare.

TENTHLY, that he shall establish a brotherhood with me on condition of obeying me in all that is good and shall keep this to the day of his death; and this relationship shall be of such a high order that the like of it shall not be found in any world relationship, either of family, or of master and servant.

Pages 178 through 185: Notes on the Meaning of Islam to a Moslem Teacher in East Africa, Predating the Eminence of the Ayatollah Ruhollah Khomeini: Or, there are Other Voices in the World of Allah.

Maulana Mubarak Ahmed is the chief of all Ahmadiyya missionaries in East Africa, with his headquarters just a desk in a tiny office behind the Ahmadiyya mosque in Nairobi, Kenya. The word *maulana* is a title, teacher. He was born in 1910 in West Punjab, at that time, northern India. Maulana Mubarak has translated the Koran into Swahili (said to be the tenth language in usage, of the world), a task he began during Ramadan, in 1936, and finished in 1953. There are over eleven hundred pages in the book, the greatest job of translation ever attempted in East Africa—perhaps all of Africa—regarding a single-volume work. Parallel to Swahili, there is the full Arabic text of the Koran. Orthodox Moslems feel that their Holy Book must never be translated without Arabic accompanying the foreign text. In case of error in translation, there is always the original version in the language of the Prophet, which has survived intact and unaltered since the seventh Christian century, when it was compiled during and shortly after Mohammed's lifetime.

Maulana Mubarak opened the first Ahmadiyya mission in East Africa, in 1934. It was ten years before another missionary joined him. He has but one wife, three daughters and one son. Funds for operating the mission are raised, by subscription, from among the local Ahmadiyya community which also underwrites the publishing costs of their literature, in English, Arabic, Swahili, Luo and Luganga. There are thirteen Pakistani missionaries under him, and twelve African. They are scattered all over East Africa, each receiving only a few shillings as monthly salaries. They are, as the Maulana says, "a very poor community . . . but we have zeal . . . we devote our lives to our assigned tasks . . . we go willingly."

A quiet, intelligent, soft-spoken man who has thought about what he wants to say, Maulana Mubarak Ahmed is a far cry from those wild-eyed Moslem fanatics, out to convert or confront the world. His job, he says, is "to lay the foundation of understanding, then others, non-Moslems, will turn to the only universal faith for all men, regardless of color, country, place in life or his community.

"They, the orthodox Moslems, feel it's a sin even to translate the Holy Koran into languages other than Arabic. But we must, for Arabic isn't universal. Unlike Christians, we have no material attractions to offer. However, if the Moslem communities of the world can only really organize, we can be of help in bringing greater balance into the world. Our duty—at the Ahmadiyya Mission—is to place before interested people an understanding of Islam, nothing more. We print long-term literature, like the Holy Koran, and short-term things like magazines, newspapers and pamphlets. Our sect is the only Islamic order trying to carry on organized Moslem missionary work. Strangely enough there are others, Moslems, who resent and oppose us.

"Islam is the future religion of Africa. We are now preparing the ground. In Islam, there is absolutely no distinction drawn between men of different skin colors, nor of race. Yes, people will come! The future struggle for Africa will be between North and South. We Ahmadiyya are in the center, from East Africa to the West. Perhaps we can achieve the balance. Coming world events will aid the spread of Islam. Thirteen hundred years ago, our Prophet spoke of the equality of all men. So to speak of racial equality, now, is just to repeat His words.

"Christianity fails in its appeal to the African for numerous reasons:

"(1): Christianity is not based upon a totally revealed Book. As years go by there are vast differences in presentation and translations. There are, admittedly, even lost sections. This creates the impression, among even less intelligent men, that the Bible is not based upon absolute, recorded fact. This is not true of the Koran, which is the same, word for word, since the first days when it was written.

"(2): What would happen if someone were to bring you a suit or the shirt of an infant to wear. Naturally, neither would fit you. The same is true of Christianity. As a religious prescription for men living during the time of Christ it was excellent. We Moslems accept these teachings, too. However, six hundred years later, Mohammed was given a more practicable prescription for the men of his time, a prescription more suited to adult civilization. The dogmas and writings of Islam will never change, for they are the revelations of the Prophet to whom God is known to have revealed His wishes. But Islam is not static. There are adequate ways in which the Koran suits itself to change and to ever-advancing social and world conditions if properly interpreted. It is here that we Ahmadiyyas find ourselves sometimes in opposition to those rigid, orthodox Moslems who believe that there can be no room for change in Islam from the first days of our Prophet Mohammed. We ask for no change in the Holy Koran, which will never change, but only ask and teach an understanding of the Koran which definitely provides for every demand in this world of today.

"(3): After research, it is our opinion that the missionary teachings of Christianity are not those of Christ, but of St. Paul. Many missionaries come to Africa with lectures which, because they represent different churches, seem to represent entirely different Bibles. This is difficult for the African to understand. While teaching a religion of suffering with Redemption later, there is every evidence that few Christians fail to struggle (as against the Mau Mau, or Communism) instead of submitting to Fate and trusting God. Such teachings are hard to believe, or to accept, and, of course, many Christians don't.

"(4): Marriage! Your wife is mad, or terribly ill, or just plain worthless (and there are some like this)— parliaments of most of the world permit you to go to the backdoor of certain houses and do bad things with other women—but you cannot marry another wife, *while caring the first*. Marry another, a second wife, openly, before God and friends! Send another generation out into the world! No! Christians deny all these things to their world. Such ideas simply don't appeal to the African, neither socially nor economically. There are fields to be worked, herds to watch, food to be prepared, young needed to care for the old. Africans are much closer to Islam than they were even ten or fifteen years ago. Natural! Practical. That is Islam!"

Pages 186 through 192: Words failed lyric poets who sought to describe it; court weavers labored for lifetimes without duplicating it; other builders recognized defeat after trying to copy it, and no one upon seeing it forgot it—only one Hand has ever succeeded in framing the beauty of the flowers-in-the-sky mosques of Isfahan, and it happens every autumn.

Pages 193 through 197: The veil: *burqa*, in Pakistan and Afghanistan, *chador*, in Iran, is still a fact of life for many women in orthodox Islamic countries like Saudi Arabia, while having almost disappeared in others like Egypt. Indonesians never adopted it, Turkish women tossed it aside (with Ataturk's blessing), and Iranians are again disappearing behind it (prodded by Khomeini)—all of which has apparently nothing whatsoever to do with the Koran, the Prophet Mohammed's admonitions, or anything other than that it simply became an accepted visible symbol of the protected but still secondary status of women, for centuries, in Islam. And yet, it perhaps was welcomed, as it provided a personal retreat from an abrasive male world when in the street. Whether rooted in assumed orthodoxy, modesty, prudence, coquettery or high fashion, the veil was/is unique in setting apart all Moslem women from the other mothers and grandmothers, peasants and housewives and career girls and queens, and flirts and virgins on earth.

In Pakistan, women have long been enmeshed in the conflict created by the direct contact of their ultra-conservative Moslem heritage with unveiled and equally conservative Hindus, the political result of which, traumatically and often hideously, was the vivisection of their homeland, British India. Although *purdah* (covering of the entire body with a draped tentlike shroud with a finely meshed peekhole or window) and the *burqa* still dominate women's dress in rural Pakistan, blending naturally and without many differences into the *burqas* of Afghanistan, voices of emancipation have long been heard and the *burqa* abandoned by many women in the largest cities. There, they participate freely, unveiled, in most urban activities—politics, publishing, the arts, medicine, and even formed the Pakistan Women's National Guard. Others, among the younger girls, cut veils from the most exotic colors and weaves, gossamer webs that jolt the heart when the eyes behind the *burqa* are laughing—making a joke of the whole thing. *(Back endpaper A)*

Page 198: (upper left) Only a few Korans remain intact from the earliest generations of Moslems, when the original Holy Book was compiled from the memories of his followers, recollections of others who knew him, and even "diaries" of Believers, some scratched on bone.

A Kufic Koran in Cairo's Museum of Islamic Art is probably the finest work of its era to survive. "Minimal art" on sacred pages. In 765, a master calligrapher thought to be Al-Imam Fa-Far as-Sadik brushed a sheen of gold on parchment, after which he painted *suras* from the Koran on otherwise unadorned pages. Then, pacing his brush as though transcribing music, he spot-placed Arabic characters in the lines of Kufic script, using a deep but vibrant red throughout the Book. The rythm created by the rising and ebbing text resembles genuflections of the Faithful praying, silhouetted against the dawn—believed, now, to have been intentional. *(paper clip indicates Koran's size)*

(upper right) In almost spectrum-splitting contrast to the Kufic Koran, *sometimes* the Islamic Museum reveals an eighteenth-century Indo-Pakistani Koran painted on the thinnest of golden leaves which themselves appear to be parchment but are almost nothing at all—the transparent skin of a hen, and the Koran itself is barely larger than a pin.

(bottom) The most precious collective treasure in the Islamic Art Museum, of course, is its luxurious array of palace carpets and prayer rugs acquired mostly through the efforts of generations of rug lovers in the ex-Royal Family. Admired and cherished since antiquity, enshrined by early Flemish then Renaissance painters, "Oriental" rugs reached the zenith of their glory as an art form in the late Middle Ages, when Kings and Pashas and Khans, Sultans and Shahs, Tzars, Medicis, and even Popes reached out beyond their thrones to touch that other realm of the artist—goldsmith-weaver-architect-painter-sculptor—to commission works in which the world would later discover that they had achieved a goal beyond the power of any earthly throne to demand but of which they all had probably dreamed . . . immortality.

As an expression of his devotion to Allah, and his feelings for the fields of wild flowers around him, an eighteenth-century Turkish Moslem ordered the weavers of Mujur to capture his emotions in hundreds of thousands of tufts of vividly dyed and knotted wool. In the center, they framed the flawless-ruby *mihrab* with wind-blown poppies, which they then framed with a meadow of sun-drenched blossoms, no two the same. During prayers, the Believer spread his magic carpet on ordinary earth, anywhere, aimed toward Mecca, knelt—and he was there.

Page 199: Moscow's May Day celebrations salute the freeing of international workers from capitalism's failings (which Soviet workers never enjoyed, being mostly ex-serfs bound to feudal-then-State lands) with endless parades of cosmonauts and off-duty firemen, factory heroes, office drones, out-of-school children, athletes and farmers and fishermen and enough soldiers and sailors and aviators and tanks and thudding boots, glistening missiles and screeching jets to give a rough idea of what it's all about in the Soviet Union, where May Day also celebrates escape from winter's grim shackles—with a nearly audible national sigh of relief. And, in total contrast to November 7, with its Revolution Day parade of mind-and-eye numbing echelons of flexed military muscle exposed to ambassadors and army attachés and world television and winter's first Arctic blasts and sometimes blizzards and the equally icy stares of those immobile silhouettes atop Lenin's and for awhile Stalin's red-and-black marble tomb, May Day in Moscow is fun, honest-to-God (even if undercover in that officially atheistic land)—fun, the highlight being horse races in the hippodrome out on the edge of town where everyone awaits the heads-to-hoofs, tunics flying, howling Cossacks who flash in and out of the stadium, leaving silence, as the chieftan of all Tadjik tribesmen in Central Asia rides ahead of his men and into each onlooker's life, glancing neither right nor left, while his horse, eyes also straight ahead and with hoofs barely touching the earth and reality, carries his master straight across that May Day carpet of painted sand and through the distant gate, back to their own world where the Russian *komissar* is still a foreigner, the Koran is still the Book—and Allah is still God. *(pages 6-7)*

Pages 200 through 227: For more than twenty-three hundred years Afghan tribesmen have fought foreign invaders who, in the end, carved their own epitaphs in the stones of dramatic but deadly places: the claustrophobic emptiness of the Dasht-i-Margo (Desert of Death), ambush-canyons of the Hindu Kush Mountains (Hindu Killer), and those over-run stone forts atop the Khyber Pass—known everywhere by that name, alone. Darius I, Alexander the Great, Moslems and Mongols, Genghis Khan, Tamerlane, Baber, Nadir Shah and other generations of Persians, then the British when they, too, coveted an Asian empire. Now, Russians, attempting to fulfill *their* centuries-old covetous dream; fighting and falling in the same mountains, dying in the same deserts, drowning in the same rivers that saw entire armies gathering along their shores with men starting across only to sink, weapons floating downstream: it all began when warriors carried spears.

King Mohammed Zahir Shah, hawk-beaked, thin, curved as a saber, stood on the Royal canopied podium watching other cavalrymen ride half-broken horses that he could have ridden better, and dancing Pushtoon tribesmen from the flanks of the Himalayas, haughty as himself, who looked him straight in the eyes while spinning and clapping to a tempo geared beyond most men, including kings. Behind Zahir Shah stood Prince Mohammed Daud, Prime Minister and brother-in-law—cannon-ball shaved, seemingly dozing, white tie, tails—Afghanistan's Independence Day—who, even then, was probably cross-checking final details of the coup that drove the King into Roman exile, ended the monarchy and cost Daud his life. He was murdered by a colleague who soon retired in "failing health" and under death threats from another colleague who disappeared but was assumed executed by *his* colleague, Babrak Karmal, now the Prime Minister of Afghanistan and recent honored guest in the Kremlin. There, as at home, he was securely cocooned within flat-faced phalanxes of Soviet bodyguards who were particularly alert when strangers approached, yet even more wary of old colleagues from Kabul, from home.

History will repeat itself. Afghanistan, country and tribesmen, will survive. All that will remain will be Cyrillic graffiti eroding among those polyglot symbols of other invaders who stormed mountains, sacked flourishing cities and mixed their conquerors' blood with that of the unconquerable—who again now fight for their homes, and stand alert over the ruins.

Pages 228 & 229: No record exists of the exact date of Mohammed's birthday: A.D. 570 has long been accepted as the year. In fact, many details of his childhood and early manhood are dimmed, or lost, by reason of his being simply another youngster of a rather remote but commercially important town—Mecca—on the caravan route linking the Mediterranean and East Africa to India. He was also half-orphaned: his father died before he was born, after which he was reared by his mother while a ward of his grandfather. By the time Mohammed was eight, his mother and grandfather were also dead and he was taken into the home of an uncle. From there he began his pilgrimage, along a route that is today revered by more than five hundred million people who live by his book, the Koran, and hold his life sacred—for he was the Prophet and Messenger of Allah . . . his words were His.

On November 8, at Muar, in Johore sultanate, Malaya, about ten thousand Moslems (half of the population of the town) celebrated the day chosen to honor the birth of the Prophet. Marchers in a parade filled the air with the staccato pounding of tambourines, topsy-turvy paper mosques mounted on rickshaws hurtled down the street with minarets already askew, unveiled ladies wearing imported silks sat quietly in parks along the route while their children ran wildly through the gardens and their men thundered out of sight.

Pages 230 through 236: When Hadji Agus Salim, "The Grand Old Man of Indonesia" died, he was buried in a cemetery reserved for military veterans and national heroes, following one of the country's rare State funerals. President and Vice-President, ambassadors of all Moslem nations and most of the others, mullahs from all the mosques, professors out of the universities, everyone, it seemed, assembled along the way to say goodbye when Hadji Salim made his final pilgrimage to Allah.

Hadji Agus Salim had made good use of his time on earth: foreign minister of his country, its foremost political thinker, independent of parties and free of bias, Islamic scholar and tolerant of all others, modest in life style, incorruptible in public life and hilarious in all the languages that he had mastered, which were many. The morning he died, his widow met the President of the Republic on the simple front porch of the Salim home while other women of the family sat in a back room with other ladies who had come to express their condolences. The men of the family—Hadji Salim's sons and brother—together with mullahs and government officials, attended the body and began traditional Moslem rites for the dead. Except for his widow and daughters, no other ladies were present.

An honor guard of four Indonesian soldiers stood beside Hadji Salim's bier during his last morning at home (orthodox Moslems must be buried within twenty-four hours of death). Ladies, friends of the Salim family, sat on the floors of adjacent rooms preparing thin shavings of sandalwood with which to scent his body, slender in its white shroud, which at first created the impression of being a Pharaonic funeral rite in Upper Egypt. After the ceremonial Islamic washing of the dead, he was draped with varying shrouds—linen and silk and luminous batik—ending with the scarlet and white flag of Indonesia. Garlands of flowers were piled upon banks of blossoms until the home and later the cemetery became tropical gardens. The mood was one of tranquility and serene dignity, and marked by profound respect among the tens of thousands of his fellow countrymen who lined the route through Djakarta leading to *Makam Pahlawan,* "Heroes Resting Place." There, his journey ended with another honor guard firing a 21-gun farewell salute, as the nation began three days of mourning.

Pages 237 through 252: The photographs should explain themselves: titles and captions are guidelines.

Back endpaper A: Pakistani girl in *burqa;* Karachi. *(page 196)*

Back endpaper B: Women at dawn prayers in Cairo, the first morning of Bairam. *(pages 112-113)*